CW00801742

At the Drop of a Miracle

Sometimes the Extravagance of God Comes a Drop at a Time

Donald Parkhill Lawrence

WESTBOW PRESS®
A DIVISION OF THOMAS NELSON & ZONDERVAN

Copyright © 2020 Donald Parkhill Lawrence.

All rights reserved. No part of this book may be used or reproduced by any means, graphic, electronic, or mechanical, including photocopying, recording, taping or by any information storage retrieval system without the written permission of the author except in the case of brief quotations embodied in critical articles and reviews.

This book is a work of non-fiction. Unless otherwise noted, the author and the publisher make no explicit guarantees as to the accuracy of the information contained in this book and in some cases, names of people and places have been altered to protect their privacy.

WestBow Press books may be ordered through booksellers or by contacting:

WestBow Press
A Division of Thomas Nelson & Zondervan
1663 Liberty Drive
Bloomington, IN 47403
www.westbowpress.com
844-714-3454

Because of the dynamic nature of the Internet, any web addresses or links contained in this book may have changed since publication and may no longer be valid. The views expressed in this work are solely those of the author and do not necessarily reflect the views of the publisher, and the publisher hereby disclaims any responsibility for them.

Any people depicted in stock imagery provided by Getty Images are models, and such images are being used for illustrative purposes only. Certain stock imagery © Getty Images.

Scripture quotations taken from The Holy Bible, New International Version® NIV® Copyright © 1973 1978 1984 2011 by Biblica, Inc. TM. Used by permission. All rights reserved worldwide.

ISBN: 978-1-6642-0270-2 (sc)
ISBN: 978-1-6642-0271-9 (hc)
ISBN: 978-1-6642-0269-6 (e)

Library of Congress Control Number: 2020915918

Print information available on the last page.

WestBow Press rev. date: 9/23/2020

I would like to dedicate this book to my wife, my children, my grandchildren, and all those who helped me along the way on my journey with Jesus.

CONTENTS

PREFACE

I am delighted to be able to share some stories with you. In fact, I am flattered that you would pick up the book, open the cover, and begin to read!

Ah! Guatemala, land of eternal springtime, land of rugged beauty, and land of twenty-eight Mayan indigenous language groups. One of these indigenous groups lives in the northeastern highlands on the north side of the Cuchumatanes mountain range. They are called the Ixil (é-sheel).

Ixil country, as it is called, encompasses about a five-hundred-square-mile area (give or take a couple of hundred miles, depending on to whom you talked) in the northern part of the *Departamento* (State) *of El Quiche*. Beautiful, rugged mountains grace the area. The area has variations of altitude from two thousand feet to nine thousand feet. It is bounded on the south by the ridges of the Cuchumatanes range and to the north by the lower Chama range. We lived in the town of Nebaj, the gateway to Ixil country.

About fifty thousand Ixil people were living in this area when we went to live among them. Their language was Maya Ixil. They were very traditional in their Mayan customs and culture, and their clothing was dazzling, elaborate, and beautiful. It was all hand woven except for the skirts, which were a dyed, bright red material. They told us the dye came from Germany. In 1975, the clothing won first prize in native costumes in the Miss Universe contest.

The first year we were there, I walked around completely

mesmerized by the beauty surrounding us. I was also captivated and, yes, intimidated by the language. I knew what challenge lay in front of me. I knew I had to learn that heart language of the Ixil if I was ever going to communicate a heart message. That part of the journey would entail years of learning!

I wish I had a little background music of the marimba to enhance the mood of the adventure we were to begin. However, on with the drop of a miracle.

I like the way C. S. Lewis put it: "Miracles are a retelling of the very same story which is written across the world in letters too large for some of us to see." This is what I am trying to do—bring those drops of a miracle into focus.

I try to relate the unexpected way that God drops a miracle on us. The experiences are set, in a way, in the ordinary. What I am trying to convey is, let's not take the ordinary for granted. I believe that God the Father wants to enhance our lives with the extraordinary, and if miracles do not do it, then I don't know what would. Obviously, we know that it is not just a drop. It is a cascading deluge overflowing with the extravagance of God the Father out of His glorious riches! He opens His glorious treasure chest and disperses as if there is no end. Jesus put it this way: "I have come in order that you might have life and have it to the full." (John 10:10).

Do not look for anything to be chronological. These are just stories patched together in a quilt of experiences. They are just stories of the incredible hand of God the Father on an ordinary family. I trust that the design comes through with Jesus Christ as the centerpiece because, you see, it is all about Him. I am encouraged to know that if He did it for us and for the people we knew, He can do it for you!

"For from Him and through Him and for Him are all things. To Him be the glory forever! Amen." (Romans 11:36)

INTRODUCTION

I consider it a privilege to be able to share in the stories. My background would not have qualified me, but by the grace of God, the Lord Jesus did the qualifying. To set the record straight I want to take a line from Saint Paul, who said, "I thank Christ Jesus our Lord, who has given me strength, that he considered me trustworthy, appointing me to His service" (1 Timothy 1:12). That is my testimony.

There is a saying that has variations, but I like the one that goes like this: "An ordinary person, sufficiently excited, can achieve an extraordinary victory." The Holy Spirit infused the excitement in me to glorify the Son Jesus with the anointing of the Father's blessing. With that kind of excitement and anointing, I applied to the International Mission Board of the Primitive Methodist Church of the USA.

I had the luxury of being sent by a mission board that gave me the great liberty to share the gospel of Jesus. I also had the great benefit of my predecessors. They set the stage with their vision. Theirs was a "wholeistic" and a holistic approach. To me, no matter how you spell it, it includes the *whole,* the totality of the person. And it includes the holistic, that point of sacredness—the holiness of the person. That is a concept of the totality of the Jesus message, to redeem the total person. Those early missionaries set the pace by addressing education, unhealthy conditions, poverty, illiteracy, and other deep social concerns.

But their overriding, deepest concern was delivering the message of Jesus in the clearest, most understandable terms. They knew that the good news of Jesus would set the people free. Yes, free indeed! In that way, they too redeemed in soul, heart, mind, and body could love, worship, and serve their Lord and God—yes, and with all of their hearts, minds, and strength!

One day, when Jesus came to the village of Nazareth, His boyhood home, He went as usual to the synagogue on Saturday and stood up to read the scriptures. The scroll of Isaiah the prophet was handed to Him, and He unrolled it to the place that says, "The Spirit of the Lord is on Me, because He has anointed me to proclaim good news to the poor. He has sent me to proclaim freedom for the prisoners and recovery of sight for the blind, to set the oppressed free, to proclaim the year of the Lord's favor." (Luke 4: 16-19) He then rolled up the scroll and handed it back to the attendant and sat down while everyone in the synagogue gazed at Him intently. Then He added, "Today this scripture is fulfilled in your hearing." (Luke 4:21)

One translation has the last phrase of the reading from Isaiah to say, "And announce that the time has come when the Lord will save his people."

Later, Saint Paul, moved by the Spirit of God, wrote,

> "Now brothers and sisters, I want to remind you of the gospel I preached to you, which you received and on which you have taken your stand. By this gospel you are saved, if you hold firmly to the word I preached to you. Otherwise, you have believed in vain.
>
> For what I received I passed on to you as the first importance: that Christ died for our sins according to the Scriptures. That He was buried, that He was raised on the third day according to the Scriptures, and that He appeared to Cephas, then to the Twelve. After that, He appeared to more than 500 of the brothers and sisters at the same time, most of

> them of whom are still living, though some of them have fallen asleep. Then He appeared to James, then to all the apostles and last of all he appeared to me also, as the one abnormally born.
>
> For I am the least of the apostles and do not even deserve to be called an apostle, because I persecuted the church of God. But by the grace of God I am what I am, and His grace to me was not without effect. No, I worked harder than all of them—yet not I, but the grace of God that was with me. Whether, then, it is I or they, this is what we preach, and this is what you have believed." (1 Corinthians 15:3–11)

This was a message of hope for the totality of the human condition. It cut across all boundaries. It is irresistible because it is centered in the very heart of God and His unconditional and incredible love.

In this message is the wonderful news that He not only declares us forgiven and not guilty, but He *makes* us not guilty. "Therefore, if anyone is in Christ, the new creation has come. The old is gone, the new is here" (2 Corinthians 5:17). It is nothing less than a "new birth" (see John 3:1–21).

It was a message that was far removed from the social gospel. It was the message preached and shared to "reverse the curse." World Vision director, Richard Stearns, in his book *Unfinished,* writes, "Jesus' words and actions represented a kind of symbolic 'turning back of the curse.'"

C. S. Lewis goes deep for us, saying, "Jesus did not come to make bad people good but to make dead people live." I would like to add my thought to that: Jesus Christ didn't come into the world to make bad people good or good people better, but He came to make men and women and boys and girls live again!

It was that message I was entrusted to deliver!

Along with the entrusted message came many opportunities to serve. One of those opportunities somewhat fell into my lap—extracting teeth. I certainly did not go looking for it. Because of the vision of the early missionaries, we had a clinic in our home. It consisted of one large room set apart to accommodate a Guatemalan nurse, an examination table, a small desk and a few chairs. There was also a small waiting room with a bench and a few chairs. The nurse had many clients, and among those were many who had toothaches. However, treating them not in her repertoire. Thus, there was a vacant spot that needed to be filled. One day early in our ministry, we had a visit from some dentists from an organization called the Flying Dentists. They did not actually fly into our area, however; they came via our road. They set up shop in our clinic and saw many patients. All of the patients were there for extractions. One day, one of the dentists said to me, "You know, you really should be doing this!" So, I looked over his shoulder as he gave me a crash course in extracting. I learned the language real fast. You don't pull teeth; you elevate them and extract them. And you don't use tools; you use instruments. I had to learn the basics real fast because he was going to be there for only two weeks. It was intense! Soon, it was his turn, and he looked over my shoulder for another week. That was more intense! He was a great teacher and coach. When it was time for him to go, he left some books and one special illustrated copy for giving the injections of the Novocain, which was priceless. And he left all of his instruments. As the years went by, other dentists came and gave me their input as well as their instruments. I even bought some of my own instruments. Toward the end, we had accumulated a vast array of instruments. Experience was a great teacher. (I almost said, "trial and error.")

We realized early on that we were treating symptoms and that we needed to get our patients on a program of dental maintenance. We strived toward that goal.

But, wait—let me get on with the stories.

CHAPTER 1

Drenched

We had a saying in our village that during the rainy season: "Not even a chicken could stand up on our streets." We were the recipients of the Caribbean clouds that blew west and got caught on our mountain range and then dumped their rain-forest precipitation on us. Those who visited our area described it as a cloud forest, but we called it a rainforest. And it rained and rained! The trails, paths, and hillsides got so wet, mossy, and slippery that we would just slip and slide and go down all over the place. It became a challenge at times to keep our balance. Some of the clay-based trails made staying upright double challenging. If you have ever seen chickens outside of the coop, I am sure you have noticed their unique ability to negotiate their terrain. Those chickens have a unique agility—they slip and slide but never lose stride. They bobble and wobble but don't go down. They get their feathers ruffled, but they seem to go along with a melodious *cluck, cluck* that seems to carry a humorous tone and projects an air of optimism that says all is well with the world. It seems to give the assurance that the chicks will be gathered under the wings and that the eggs will be laid and hatched. But even this agility meets its match on the hilly slopes of Ixil country. So when we slipped, we did not have to feel too bad—why, even a chicken couldn't stand up there! I think the results and the challenges of those rainy seasons inspired the title *At the Drop of a Miracle.*

I know that you have experienced a day in summer that is so, so hot and humid. The sultry heat is almost oppressive. But you seem to sense that relief is in store. Then, off in the distance, you see the ominous dark clouds and hear the roll of thunder. There are the majestic lighting flashes, and the next thing you know the storm is upon you. Ah—the refreshing rain falls and seems to pull you into its presence. You step out and let the rain spatter your upturned face. You soak up the raindrops as they sprinkle your face. And then it is gone. It came so quickly that it almost caught you off guard, and now the sun is already poking through the black-gray clouds. An eerie steam vapor is emanating from the ground, as is a restorative breath of earthy freshness. It is cool. It feels good to be alive. You have just experienced a miracle. Those drops pattering on your forehead were "drops of a miracle."

I had one of those experiences one day; however, it was on a different scale. It was one of those oppressively hot and humid eastern Pennsylvania summer days. Relief was coming in the form of a dramatic thunderstorm. I stood on the porch of the house two hundred yards from the church to observe the special effects of the storm and was not disappointed as the thunder rolled and the lighting flashed. The special effects were impressive. The rain was still coming down when I thought that I heard the sound of a siren in the distance. Why, yes, it was a siren, and it seemed to be coming my way. I thought I'd better make a run for it to see if everything was all right at the church. As I approached the church parking lot, I saw what looked like someone lying in the parking lot. Evidently, someone else must have seen the same thing and called 9-1-1. I ran up to the body and found a young girl, fully clothed, lying spread-eagle, face up on the blacktop making "rain angels". By the side of the parking lot was her car, with the driver-side door still open. When she became aware that I was looking down at her and heard the screeching siren at our side, she stopped her flapping. As the EMS personnel approached, she sat up and said, "What's going on?"

"Hey, that's our question," I said.

Then she began to explain. "Driving in the drenching downpour after such oppressive heat I just could not resist. I saw this nice, vacant, gently sloping parking lot. *Ah*, I thought, *I'll just step out and enjoy a few moments of sheer enjoyment in the rain*. And what better way than to spread out here on my back, face in the rain and the warmth of the asphalt on my back—what a moment!" And now we all stood for a moment to take in what we just heard. We reflected on the spontaneity, the exuberance, and the impulsiveness of youth to take a moment to enjoy life—and the drop of a miracle!

Sometimes the rains come like that. They almost catch you unawares. Then there are the times when the rains come when predicted. The forecast says there will be rain, and it may last for days. Those good ol' nor'easters illustrate the word *storm*. Those rains come and last for days—in fact, you wonder if it will ever stop. If you are caught at sea, you wonder if you will survive. Those, too, are drops of miracles. They hint of the extravagance of God and accomplish their purpose.

Sometimes the rain comes at night, almost secretly, doing its duty and moving on. You were unaware, so when you awaken, you realize, "Oh, it rained last night." Those were drops of a miracle nonetheless because the results they will produce have already begun to take effect.

I like to think of these drops of a miracle as something only God can do. They come into our lives, and just like the rain they accomplish their purpose. They leave behind the wherewithal to produce life, growth, and a harvest. They produce a sense of hope.

The experiences that we share through the following pages brought a great refreshing, encouragement, and challenge to our lives. I can only hope that as you read through these pages, you too will be refreshed, encouraged, and challenged.

So, lift up your head and tilt it to the sky—to the hills—and to the Lord, from where your help really comes, expecting a miracle. It might come in dramatic form when you least expect it. It might come out of a consistent, driving force of the drama of the kingdom of God. And it might come without your being aware until it begins to affect your life and the lives of those around you.

Drops of a miracle—how desperately we need them and how extravagantly God gives them. Obviously, we know that it is not just a drop of a miracle but a cascading, overflowing deluge of the extravagance of God our Father that He pours down on us. And that deluge is filled with His mercy, goodness, grace, and love.

So read on, my fellow traveler, pilgrim, co-laborer, and fellow soldier. And, oh yes, don't forget your poncho, raincoat, and umbrella. Oh, never mind, forget them—just go on and get soaked in the glorious, lavish riches of God. Enjoy!

CHAPTER 2

Knock, Knock—Who's There?

"Knock, knock."

"Who's there?"

"Yoshio."

"Who?"

"Yoshio who lost three!"

"Three what?"

Thus, the conversation and adventure began on that Saturday morning.

Our house was Spanish style with a ten-foot corridor that was the entrance into the patio and the house area. We had a nice wooden door, so a knock on the door echoed and magnified through the corridor. It could even draw you out of bed!

Imagine having no house phone, no cell phone, and no Internet—that door was our connection to the world. We were never sure what part of the world we were going to encounter behind that door.

This particular Saturday morning, I confronted a young Japanese man. He was typical of the young people of the sixties and seventies who were traveling the world. This young traveler wore the typical uniform of those days—a faded pair of jeans and a shabby, short-sleeve sweatshirt. I'm sure you can imagine what they looked like.

Yoshio, in halting English, began to share with me that he had lost something. When he began to speak, I knew that we were in trouble—not just in trouble because he had lost something but also in the area of lost communication. His English was not that good, he could not speak Spanish, and my Japanese ended with *sayonara*. So we picked English, and with some signs thrown in, Yoshio began to share with me what he had lost.

Holding up three fingers he said, "Lost three!"

I replied, "Three what—three friends, three dollars, three hundred, three thousand?"

"Ah! Yes," he said excitedly, "three thousand!"

And the story began to unfold. He had kept the money in a money belt (supposedly). He had spent Friday night in another town over the mountain range. Before dawn on Saturday morning, he caught a truck for the four-hour ride to our town. When he arrived, he discovered that he did not have his money anymore—what a shocker! Somehow during that trip he had lost his money, or someone had relieved him of it. During his anguished wanderings on our town streets, someone pointed him toward our house.

I looked at Yoshio and said, "I don't know if you can understand this or not, but there is a word in English that signifies what you need. That word is *miracle*! A miracle is something only God can do. I'll pray with you, and I'll help you as best I can, but I know that it is only going to be God who can help you recover this money."

So we began the search. The first logical place to look was the truck. We looked in every nook and cranny of the truck—nothing. I did notice, however, that the doors did not close tightly; in fact, there were gaps. Could it have been that, through all the bouncing, bumping, and jostling as they traveled along the road, the money could have slipped out and fallen through the gaps? It was just an idea, but why not backtrack up the road? We decided to give it a try. We snaked our way up the mountain road, scanning the roadway. About an hour into the trip, we arrived at the country store and restaurant where they had eaten breakfast. There were coffee and corn bags everywhere, including the dining area. Yoshio remembered that he had stretched out on some of the bags to relieve some of the kinks in his back as he waited for the driver and helper to finish their breakfast. We moved every bag and gave them a thorough search—no money. I thought it was best that we head back to town.

But I had one more idea. What about a search of the driver and helper? After all, everyone could be under suspicion. The Guatemalan army had a garrison stationed in our town, and I had made a couple of friends in their ranks. I was reluctant to do this, but I was about to test my *cuello* (influence). I spoke to them about the problem, and they immediately rounded up the driver and his helper and gave them a thorough shakedown—nothing.

Each moment that the search continued, the more skeptical I became. Grave doubts were dancing around in my head. *Did he really have the money? Is he spaced out on drugs?* He sort of looked like he might be! What was he trying to get out of me?

By now it was getting dark. Now I had to loan him some money, feed him, and find a place for him to stay. Well, God, no drop of a miracle yet!

We got together Sunday morning and rehashed the situation. I perceived the situation as having run the course of all the options of finding the money in our town. I kind of decided to give up. However, I had one last idea and asked Yoshio one last question.

"When was the last time that you can remember that you were actually sure of the money—you saw it, handled it, and counted it?"

"You know what?" Yoshio said (I am loosely translating his broken English, but I got the gist). "I do remember counting the money on Friday night in the room at the pension where I was staying."

Sunday was a huge market day in our town, and people came

from all over to flood the plaza area, which meant there was transportation galore. A light went on for me.

"Ah!" I said to Yoshio. "I think that you should return to Uspantan and get back to that boarding house. There is a bus leaving right now at the plaza for Uspantan."

I saw Yoshio catch the crowded bus, and he was on his way. *Oh well*, I thought, *I did the best I could.*

The next day, I left on a trip out of town to go to our hospital in Chichicastenango, which is about a four-hour drive from our town. About an hour from our town, we drop off the mountain range and wind another half an hour down into a river valley. Along this river valley are scattered villages. One town, Sacapulas, has the claim to fame because it has a bridge, which makes it the focal point for converging traffic. Anyone going north or south or east or west has to cross over this bridge. It is also a nice spot to take a break, with beautiful, full mango trees and roadside stands with an array of food and hawking vendors. It makes for a refreshing stop.

When we arrived in Sacapulas at about noon, a bus pulled in right behind us. As I got out of my car, I noticed a young Japanese man literally leaping out of the bus. He was ecstatic and came running toward me, shouting, "I found it! I found it!"

"Oh?" I said in disbelief. "Tell me about it."

In an elaborate display of arms and hand signs, a flow of English, Spanish and Japanese we began to decipher and piece together Yoshio's story. It seemed that as soon as he got off the bus in Uspantan he went straight to the boarding house. He asked the cleaning girl to let him into the room where he had slept. It seems at that moment he had that moment of flashback that he had taken the money out of the money belt and put it in the pillowcase. The next morning, he jumped up in haste to catch the bus, gabbed his money belt and forgot the money! In a panic, he raced across the room to the bed and grabbed the pillowcase. Wow, would you believe this? When he picked up the pillowcase and looked inside, there was his money!

Thank you, Jesus, for the drop of a miracle!

When Yoshio discovered his money, he said he immediately peeled off a hundred-dollar bill and gave it to the cleaning lady for not changing the linens.

When he finished telling his story, I offered to give him a ride. He got into the car, and my curiosity got the best of me. I asked, "Yoshio would you show it to me?"

And sure enough, he peeled off his money belt and fanned through twenty-nine one-hundred-dollar bills!

Now the fascinating part of this story is that two men had slept in that room the Saturday night after Yoshio departed for our town. They never discovered the money. I could just imagine this one fellow sleeping in the bed with his head on the pillow and feeling a lump on the side of his head. He would grumble in his sleep, growl about the accommodations, and then flip the pillow over to get the soft, cool side, when he would find that he was sleeping on three thousand dollars! Every time I think of this story, I think of my own spiritual life. How many times have I been dozing and, yes, even sound asleep on top of the riches and resources of my Father? And I bet that if you were to think hard enough, you can remember some of the times that you were asleep too. We grumble, we toss and turn, and we turn the pillow of life over to get the cool, soft side of our own selfish desires, our own power, our own comfort zones—whatever—and we sleep on. And we get our own puny results. Then we wonder why we are so shallow and weak. We have not taken into account the mighty power and resources of our Father. Oh, our Father has something better and greater in store for us. "Wake up, O sleeper, rise from the dead, and Christ will shine on you" (Ephesians 5:14).

I trust that the story of Yoshio will remind us that our Father has unlimited treasure at our disposition. He wants us to take advantage and appropriate what is truly ours. He wants us to conscientiously shake off the cobwebs of lethargy and become more alive. I trust that the Father will continue to encourage us to tap into His glorious riches.

May that eureka, that epiphany moment be yours and mine as the Holy Spirit unlocks the divine splendor in you and me!

Oh, yes, one other thought. I found it amazing how much Yoshio and I could communicate through improvised charades and feeble attempts at sign language. There were even a few moments when we used words.

And now, I have this quirky habit. Every hotel or motel that I stay in, I look into and shake out each pillowcase.

CHAPTER 3

Whatcha Got Under the Bed?

Casico heard the good news about Jesus, was touched by the Spirit, made a decision, and believed. Casico's decision to become a follower of Jesus did not go unnoticed in the small Ixil village of Pulay, which was nestled in the rugged terrain about fifteen kilometers northeast of our town of Nebaj. In fact, his decision stirred quite a discontent among his friends and neighbors in the community. It was as if one of the star players had switched teams. On one side, the Christian community was encouraged, and on the other side, those of the strong indigenous religious system were somewhat dismayed.

Strong Maya Ixil religious practices make it very difficult for individuals to make a break from their strong ties. In fact, in many instances, social and family ties are broken by this decision for Jesus. The Maya Ixil religious system and worship permeates every facet of Ixil society. The networking and connections are very strong. The religious system is led by and shepherded by an array of religious practitioners who are held in high esteem and hold sway over the communities.

The religious practitioners keep account of the days of the Mayan calendar, spiritual accounts with the spirit world, and the account with the ancestors. They can heal, cast spells, block curses, interpret dreams, and do whatever else needs attention in the spirit world. And Casico was part of that world. He did not hold high rank, but he was in the ranks nonetheless. Casico was also advanced in age, and that was another plus for his credentials in Ixil society. His grandfatherly posture gave him a tip of the hat in society.

But Casico believed in Jesus and became a follower of the Jesus way. He took the risk of being ostracized. He also knew that any kind of a hint or shadow of doubt over his new life would be overmagnified by the other side. They would take no sympathy for the veneration of age nor his former status among the religious leaders. In fact, they might very well use those facts against him.

A test of Casico's faith came sooner than anyone expected. A few months into his new walk in Christ, we were in for a vivid demonstration of "and we know that in all things God works for the good of those who love Him and are called according to His purpose" (Romans 8:28). Casico fell deathly ill!

The word spread quickly. And here they came—those religious practitioners I spoke about. They could hardly wait to show up, and show up they did!

"Casico," they said, "have you lost your mind? What were you thinking? Why would you turn your back on the real gods and follow this strange, foreign god? Well, it serves you right for abandoning the true gods! Oh, Casico, turn back. Turn back before it is too late!" It was like a frightening crescendo of choruses as the parade of visitors marched into and out of Casico's home.

Casico's son, Thomas, was witness to all that was going on, and he became deeply burdened with concern. *Where can I go for some help?* he thought. He journeyed to our town, shared with us his anxieties, and asked if there was anything we could do. We immediately replied, "Of course." I said, "We can go to see your father and pray for him, and we'll take some medicine and just see how serious the situation is."

We left town immediately in the Land Rover and traveled the fifteen kilometers to Thomas and Casico's thatched-roof home. When we arrived at the house, we found that, indeed, Casico was deathly ill. He shared with us that he was experiencing high fever and had a great deal of severe discomfort. He told us he had had a parade of visitors. He also retold some of the comments emphasizing the spiritual battle.

"Serves you right," they had said. "Go running off to serve another god. No wonder you are sick. You have forsaken our true gods and spirits, and now you are being punished. Come back! Come back so that your soul can be guarded by our spirits. Come back before it is too late. Come back!"

What a tremendous spiritual, emotional, and physical struggle was going on. What could we do?

We spent some time in prayer and felt the nudging of the Spirit of God to move Casico to our partnership-in-mission hospital in Chichicastenango. We bundled Casico in his blankets and tenderly loaded him in the Land Rover. There was a five-hour ride ahead over a dusty, bumpy, marimba-etched road.

We drove southwest and felt a refreshing "drop of a miracle." Casico's and his family's willingness to go out of Ixil country for treatment represented a breakthrough. Many, many Ixil believe that hospitals and doctors have no more control over curing illness than the simplest peasant. The Ixil believe that those who possess real power are the Ixil religious practitioners, who hold sway in the spirit world. Suppose you died outside of Ixil country—what happened to your soul? So Casico's willingness to go demonstrated his confidence in his new God—Jesus!

We arrived at the hospital and surrendered Casico to the Lord Jesus and the capable, professional care of the hospital staff. When we drove off that evening and headed toward home, we had no idea what was in store for Casico and the Ixil community.

We were anxious to hear a report on Casico's progress, and little by little reports drifted in of his physical improvement. Finally, the day came when Casico was released from the hospital. He was physically strong enough to board a bus to begin his journey back home.

The bus route took him through our town, so Casico stopped off to see me. I was delighted to see him looking so well, so healthy. Indeed, he had improved dramatically! However, I noticed that something seemed to be troubling him. Casico began to share.

He revealed that his life had fallen under great conviction. I could see that what he was about to disclose with me was high-priority business.

"Sure," he began, "I had accepted Jesus and I knew that Jesus had taken hold on my heart and some of my life. But I had been hedging on an important issue. That issue was, and is, total surrender to Jesus Christ as Lord of all! The Holy Spirit had in effect said to me, 'What have you got under the bed'?"

Casico continued, "Well, you see, even though Jesus and His Word came into my heart very strong and even though I had mouthed the words and believed in my heart, I just did not feel strong enough in my spirit to take any chances! You see, all those years delving in powerful spirit worship, dream interpretation, divination, and white, gray, and black magic were so connected and were so, so difficult to let go. So, I said to myself—why, I'll just hide a few gods and talismans under the bed just in case."

"But now, because of the Holy Spirit's Word, it all had to go." Then Casico said to me, "Will you get together as many believers as you can and come out to my house on Tuesday? I'm going to burn up all my idols."

"Praise the Lord," I said. "I'll be delighted to do so!"

Tuesday dawned with regal mountain splendor in our town. Tuesday also dawned with the same splendor in Pulay—except an eerie shroud seemed to hang over the Casico residence. There were misgivings, hedging, doubts, and fear. *Am I doing the right thing?* seemed to be the unspoken thoughts. We could feel a foreboding hanging over the area as we drove into Pulay. When we arrived at Casico's house, we could see that he was upset. It seemed that his wife, children, and grandchildren were also uneasy and upset. But we had come based on Casico's decision a few days before. We had arrived. We were all together and connected, and then, suddenly, nothing seemed stronger than our Christian camaraderie. That bonding brought about encouragement and reinforcement of decisions — "a drop of a miracle!"

We prayed, shared some personal testimonies of the power of our God, and shared encouragement from God's Word. There was an infusion of spiritual courage—and the shroud lifted!

"Let's go through with it!" Casico almost shouted.

Then Casico and his son went into the house to gather all of the images, idols, and talismans and brought them out. Even a few wooden crosses were tossed in.

A few dried cornstalks flamed up around some kindling, and soon we had a blaze going. And then, with a ritual type tossing, the items were thrown into the fire. The regal splendor of the day became even more spectacular. Now, as the fire began to consume the items, we began to feel a special sense of relief and victory. It was as if the fire was consuming and dissipating doubt and unbelief.

As the fire burned down, we noticed that one of the wooden idols had not burned completely. It was charred like alligator skin and still smoldering. Pap Lap, the Ixil evangelist, stabbed it with his machete and lifted it out of the fire. Then he proceeded to chop the idol into kindling. A piece splintered off into the air and fell at our feet. Immediately, one of Casico's grandsons picked it up and showed it to his grandfather.

"Look, Granddad," he said. "Look, it is just like a piece of wood, just like grows in the forest and like we use for cooking!"

Yes, it was just another piece of wood. But that piece of wood, just like the other things that had been tossed into the fire, had taken on an eerie aspect of power. They were coy and powerful counterfeits enhanced by the evil one for the real thing. Just as he always has done from the beginning by deceit, lies, and spiritual intimidation, he tries to pull men and women away from the true God, Creator, and Savior. This Tuesday, however, he was defeated by the awesome power of the One and only true God—Father, Son Jesus, and the Holy Spirit.

What happened on that Tuesday was spoken about so, so long ago. God's spokesman said it so clearly: "Yes, men do feed on ashes indeed!" (For the whole context see Isaiah 40:1–40.)

What do *you* have under the bed? May God help us all to make that critical, decisive, and life-changing decision to make Jesus Lord of all.

We were made to put God first. Anything that takes away your love and loyalty to God is an idol. They come in all types, shapes, and sizes—power, pleasure, money, fame, the NFL, or something out of wood. The categories are endless.

We were made to put God first. And what if we don't? God's Word tells us that we become like our idols; we become what we worship. This is what God's Word says: "What fault did your fathers find in me that they strayed so far from me? They followed worthless idols and became worthless themselves" (Jer. 2:5).

Saint Augustine was once accosted by someone who was hostile to the Christian faith, who showed him his idol and said, "Here is my god. Where is yours?" Augustine replied, "I cannot show you my God, not because there is no God or that God does not exist but because you have no eyes to see Him!"

And it was that legendary Saint Augustine who wrote, "Thou hast made us for thyself, O God, and restless are our hearts until they rest in Thee."

As I reflected over some of the events of Casico's life, I began to think of some of the situations that he faced. You know, he could have said to those people who came down so hard on him, "Hey, wait a minute. I still have a lot of stuff under the bed. And it is powerful stuff too!" And he would have been back in good graces. No, Casico didn't throw in the towel when things looked so bad.

Isn't it wonderful how the Lord Jesus sustains us in our trials?

His words, "I will never leave you or forsake you," are for real! We get a two-fold promise.

Divided by doubt and the thoughts of not wanting to take any chances, I am sometimes in the Casico mode. I get caught up in a two-fold heart. There is that divided heart that knows but is reluctant to act. I am thankful for the touch of the Holy Spirit that reassures me and draws me back to a more powerful "belief"! The day-to-day adventure becomes filled with victories and the "drops of a miracle" because of Him. What do you have under the bed?

CHAPTER 4

A Burst of Divine Splendor Arched across the Ixil Countryside

Esteban had quite a job— he was both a lumberjack and a carpenter. He did what lumberjacks do; he went to the forest and chopped trees down. These lumberjacks, however, sawed the logs up right there in the woods. They built a lean-to ramp structure into the mountainside and rolled the logs onto the open ramp assembly. There was standing room under the open bay. A two-man crosscut saw was put into use, with one man on the top and one on the bottom. They sawed the log lengthwise into manageable planks, which were then lugged to the carpenter shop to dry. Esteban had an assortment of formations of drying, rough lumber outside of his shop. When the wood was dry, Esteban would make beams, planks, boards, and two-by-fours out of the rough lumber. Out of that wood, he would make an array of things—houses, furniture, truck bodies, truck racks, and whatever else the townsfolk ordered. Esteban, along with this labor-intense job, also had another crucial job. He was one of the chief idol makers. Yes, out of this same wood that he worked with day in and day out, he made and fashioned idols. His reputation was widespread.

On an ordinary night after a hard day's work, Esteban went to bed. On this ordinary night, something dramatic was about to happen. Esteban had a dream that would change his life forever. The dream was so real and vivid that he could recount every detail.

This is the way Esteban recounts it:

> The dream was a life-and-death situation. Death, torment, and destruction were stalking me! I ran from the situation to escape and find freedom from the horror. As I ran I came to the end of the road and encountered a raging river—and to add to the eerie intrigue it was a river of blood! I stopped and suddenly realized that there was no escape except through the river. But I also sensed that there was on the other side of the river a calm, strong atmosphere of freedom and safety. But I thought, *How I am ever going to get across?* No one could survive that torrent and those swirling undercurrents. I would be swept away—and to where? There was a huge foreboding of what those consequences would be. But what was I to do? Death, destruction, and torment were closing in.

"Wait!" I said to myself. "I have an idea! I'll call my idols. They have power. They will get me across."

> So I called for my idols. They came, and they sounded like the cavalry arriving in the nick of time.

> "Whoa!" they said when they arrived. "Wow, look at that river!"
>
> I began to beg them and plead with them to get me across the river, and pronto! A couple of brave idols timidly tested the waters. "Oh," they said, "no way!"
>
> Death was about to engulf us, and I was beside myself. In desperation, I cried out, "What am I going to do? Who can help me?"
>
> Then suddenly, from the other side of the bank of the river, out of the mist, there appeared a figure. A glow and a tug of spiritual ecstasy emanated from the figure. The shrouded figure waded into the river and began to cross. There was a mystical, ghostlike clouding of the figure, and yet a brilliance and an aura shrouded his movements. I was uncontrollably drawn to it. There was a sense that it was and is good—yes, yes, very, very good. It was irresistible. The river seemed to rage even more as it moved across it to move toward my side of the river. The figure emerged from the river and approached me. The figure reached out and touched me, and I thought I would melt. Before I knew it I was hoisted on the figure's back and carried—it actually seemed like we glided across the river. When we reached the other side and were about to emerge from the river, suddenly I awakened.

Esteban was deeply troubled by the dream and he began to wonder who was going to be able to help him interpret this dream.

The next morning, as Esteban was on his way to the woods, he overheard a conversation between two men. They were talking about a new person who was in the town jail.

Apparently, a traveling preacher had been roaming the countryside sharing the Gospel of Jesus Christ. Many of the folks were upset with him and asked the mayor to have him put in jail and then kicked out of town. The new person in jail was that itinerant preacher waiting to get escorted out of town. When Esteban heard this news, he felt drawn to seek him out. *Maybe this is a man of God*, Esteban thought, *and he can help me interpret my dream!* So Esteban hurried off to the local jail.

The jail was part of the town hall building complex, and there was easy access to the prisoners. Huge, thick, wooden doors barred three cells. Once inside those doors, Esteban had no trouble finding the new prisoner, and he began to share with this roving evangelist the story of his dream. It did not take the evangelist long to catch the spiritual implications, and he said, "Esteban, without a doubt the One who came across the river for you was none other than the Lord Jesus Christ Himself!"

"Woe is me!" cried Esteban. "What am I to do?"

"Ah," said the evangelist, "what a great sign for you. The Lord Jesus shed His blood for you and died for you! He did that because He loves you. He will cleanse you from all sin and give you a clean heart and carry you into heaven. Don't be afraid because He will carry you through the turbulent waters of life. He did what none of your idols could ever do. Believe on Him now!"

Esteban fell on his knees, and a prisoner on the other side of the bars was set free. What irony—there in prison Esteban was set free. From that moment on, he had no doubt about his delivery from the kingdom of terror, darkness, and death into God's marvelous love, life, light, and freedom.

After this encounter with Jesus, Esteban continued to climb upward to new spiritual levels. One occasion that is so vivid to me is when I had the privilege to travel with Esteban to one of our congregations on a coffee plantation. In the years prior to our visit, he had sold many of his handmade idols to various families living there. Now, he went from house to house telling the people that the idols he had made were really nothing. He encouraged the people to never put confidence in an idol and what it represented. What an experience it was, traveling with him into the homes and hearing his story. Esteban shared his faith in Jesus as the one and only true God. He encouraged the people to turn from idols and spiritual darkness to serve the true and living God of love and light.

One evening on the plantation Esteban was asked to share his testimony. The leaders of the church also asked me to preach. Can you imagine being on the same program with a man like Esteban? His testimony was strong and powerful. I really didn't think it was necessary for me to preach when he finished; nevertheless, I rose to my feet. The Holy Spirit's special pervading made everything flow with power. It was a special night.

Esteban continued to serve and be used by the Lord Jesus in a special way. Included in God's blessings in his life was a dramatic healing. One day in the woods as he and his son were rolling a log toward the lean-to, they began to slip and the log started to roll out of control. Esteban noticed the danger to his son. He reached frantically for the leverage pole, and with an extra burst of strength that stretched and pushed every sinew and ligament to their limits, the leverage pole held! Esteban and his son had escaped disaster. But Esteban was left with excruciating pain in his groin area. He began to double over from the intense pain. It seemed as if he had experienced a double hernia. His son struggled and was able to get his father draped over a horse and headed for home. When they arrived at the house, Esteban shuffled to a hammock. He swayed into the hammock and tried to rest. (I am not sure that being draped over a horse and canoed in a hammock is the best first response for a hernia.) Nevertheless, Esteban tried to rest. He wondered what he was to do, so he prayed for healing. And there as he lay in the hammock, he had a visitation from Jesus. The appearance of the majestic figure was just as real as it had been in his dream of the river of blood. Jesus touched Esteban, and he was immediately healed!

Well, you know that the evil one, Satan, was not at all happy at what was happening. He mustered an all-out attack with the powers of the rulers of darkness and the spiritual forces of evil at his disposal. It was a three-pronged attack on Esteban's marriage, social position, and work.

Satan's attack was brutal and devastating. Esteban began to have marital problems. Many of the townsfolk refused to buy from him or give him work, and he was ostracized by his neighbors. These attacks overwhelmed Esteban, finally reaching a point that he decided to move to another town.

Esteban came to our town and told us of his decision to move and to try to start over. The embarrassment of his marriage, the lack of work, and the estrangement of his family and neighbors had taken their toll. It was a vivid remembrance—Esteban walking down our street with his few possessions to the bus stop. I did not hear much from him in the next few months. Then it seemed that Esteban just faded away and dropped out of sight and sound.

"Esteban, Esteban, where are you?" I cry out.

Today there is a strong, thriving evangelical community in Esteban's former town. Could it be that it is the result of the seeds that Esteban sowed and then God the Father touched to produce the growth and fruit? Yes, those early sacrifices of Esteban now are producing fruit—good fruit, solid fruit. And that fruit is in turn producing the seeds for more growth and fruit by the Spirit.

"Oh, Esteban, where are you? Come back, Esteban. Come back to your old village and see what the Holy Spirit has done!" I plead.

Maybe somewhere Esteban is waiting for that drop of a miracle. God would surely shower it down upon him again, and there would be great spiritual victory. And once again a brilliant flash would arc across the Guatemalan countryside.

We are in a spiritual warfare, a spiritual opposition about which Martin Luther said, "If the right man was not on our side, we would be losing." Thank God, the right Man is on our side! Oh, sure, there are going to be some defeats, and some of them may be bitter. We don't intentionally look for or expect defeat, but we obviously need to be on our guard, as the Holy Spirit inspired Paul to say,

> "Finally, be strong in the Lord and his mighty power. Put on the whole armor of God so that you can stand against the devil's schemes. For our struggle is not against flesh and blood, but against the rulers, against the authorities, against the powers of this dark world and against the spiritual forces of evil in the heavenly realms. Therefore put on the full armor of God, so that you may be able to stand your ground, and after you have done everything, to stand. Stand firm then, with the truth buckled round your waist, with the breastplate of righteousness in place and with your feet fitted with the readiness that comes from the gospel of peace. In addition to all of this, take up the shield of faith, with which you can extinguish all the flaming arrows of the evil one. Take the helmet of salvation and the sword of the spirit, which is the word of God. And pray in the Spirit on all occasions with all kinds of prayers and requests. With this in mind, be alert and always keep on praying for all the saints." (Ephesians 6:10–18)

Has God been speaking to you? I know that nothing takes the place of His Word. Dreams surely don't. But who is to say that Esteban's dream was not valid? It seems to me that the Father is still at work and sometimes uses special effects to get our attention. Well, why not? "In the last days," God says,

> "I will pour out My Spirit on all people. Your sons and daughters will prophesy, your young men will see visions, your old men will dream dreams. Even on my servants, both men and women, I will pour out My Spirit in those days and they will prophesy. I will show wonders in the heavens above and signs on the earth below, blood and fire and billows of smoke. The sun will be turned to darkness and the moon to blood before the coming of the great and glorious day of the Lord. And everyone who calls on the name of the Lord will be saved." (Acts 2:17–18)

So, has He been speaking to you through his Word by the power of Holy Spirit? Listen to that voice and remember that we win—because of Jesus!

CHAPTER 5

The Cement Block Plant

I was the mission board's field director at the time of the earthquake and wrote about some of the experiences of those first days. Being the field director, I had to immediately move into the phase of first responding. We quickly formed a committee with the national conference and the US conference, and we called it the Committee of Reconstruction Evangelical Methodists, with CREM serving as our acronym. We had wonderful cooperation from the Guatemalan government. They gave us a full range of liberties and backed it up with stamps of authority.

In those early days of the first response, I had the privilege to work alongside don Juan Par of the national conference. It was a great blessing to work with a man of such deep spiritual sensitivity, humble spirit, and great integrity.

Obviously, those first days were the days of intense priorities. Burying the dead, taking care of all the injured, and getting food and other supplies to the people were the first items on our list. Of course, shelter was a prime issue also. We needed to get roofs over their heads. We began a program that distributed tin roofing. So much was needed; that alone was a job in itself.

The wonderful thing was to see the great response of all the people in the United States. The US Government sent a lot of equipment for reconstruction of the roads and the bridges. That was an urgent and critical need. They also flew in, as I mentioned in my other chapter, through the use of the Chinook helicopters food and other supplies to some of the isolated villages. The people in US churches were so, so generous. What a blessing—we seemed to have not just adequate but an abundance of funds. Little by little, things began to improve. Then, we realized that an immense reconstruction agenda was ahead of us. We also realized that we needed to bring about changes in the construction of homes and churches to give them more stability. We needed to reinforce the adobe. And after a study, it seemed to us that the ideal method would be reinforced concrete-block construction.

Could it be possible to build a block plant of our own? We began to pursue the idea, and then it became a vision. What a blessing it could be if we had our own concrete block plant. Whoa! Were we thinking too big here? Then faith stepped in. Who is our God? Is there anything too hard for Him? And just then we realized that two members of our churches in the United States owned block plants. The vision became a reality! We immediately began to pick their brains about the possibility of building a concrete block plant in Guatemala. The answer came back, "Of course!" They sent along a requirements list: sand (plenty of it), water, electric power, and cement. They presumed that we could muster the labor force. As the vision became more of a reality, the committee sent me to the United States to check out the feasibility and possibility of getting a block plant to Guatemala. I met with the leaders of our International Mission Board, and they were on board with the vision. We then met with the owners of the block plants. We went to the actual concrete block plant, and I was overwhelmed. The owners began to share with us and said, we will be able to ship to you one of our block plants. It will consist of all the components that you will need. There will be a huge mixing bin with the mixing paddles, the conveyor belts, the electric motors, all the pipes, steel girders and beams and the control panels. This array of materials will make the same configuration of machinery that you see here. It will need a strong concrete foundation as an anchor for the machinery. When it all comes together, as assembled, it will mix, vibrate, mold and compress for you a finished product—a cement block. It will require a lot of preventive maintenance to keep it running. It was, in a sense, a mobile cement block plant that we were going to have to assemble in Guatemala. As I stood there, I tried to take it all in. It was difficult to wrap my head and heart around the realization that it all could be possible.

A wave of doubt washed over me, and I thought, *There is no way that this block plant will ever get to Guatemala*. But the more we talked and prayed and were prodded by the Holy Spirit, the more we felt led to do it. Meanwhile, I was dealing with the echo of, "Oh, you of little faith." So, bathed in prayer, we began to put the process in motion.

The first thought was that we could ship all the machinery of the concrete block plant on an eighteen-wheeler. After we pursued the details of the possibility of trouble through the United States and in Mexico, and especially taking into consideration some of the low-arched bridges, we had to make some decisions. We finally decided that it would be best to ship the block plant by cargo ship. So we began to make those arrangements. Meanwhile, I returned to Guatemala to find a suitable place for the plant, all the while remembering the phrase "a lot of sand."

After the earthquake, we had been moved out of our hometown of Nebaj for practical purposes and to the town of Chichicastenango. It was more centrally located in the area. I came back from the block plant project discussion and planning in the States, and we decided to travel back to our hometown of Nebaj to see how things were going there. We traveled through the town of Sacapulas to get home. (Remember the revealing of the twenty-nine one-hundred-dollar bills?) This time, as I drove through that valley to the town, all I saw were banks of sand. *Could it be that this is where the block plant should go?* And, oh, by the way, there's a river flowing right through the town! To check off another priority on our list, a whole new electric power line grid had just been completed a few years earlier that ran through the town. We began to pray and pursue the town officials of Sacapulas. With all of the credentials and the backing of the Guatemalan government, it was very easy to convince them to give up a very choice piece of land right by the river, right by tons of sand and everything else that we needed. (Oh, you of doubt and of little faith!)

Now came the adventure of getting the block plant through the waves of the Atlantic and the Caribbean to the docks of Guatemala and over the mountainous roads to Sacapulas. Meanwhile, we had to lay the groundwork for receiving the block plant. We needed access to water, electricity, sand, and of course a workforce. The president of the national conference that year was don Salomon Hernandez, a wonderful person with whom to work. In a sense he was God's man for the hour. We worked in close collaboration on all the details of getting the concrete block plant set up. Through the generosity of a Grand Rapids, Michigan, church, we had a brand-new Ford pickup for the "go for." Through the generosity of many other believers, we had at our disposal two other larger trucks to haul materials.

Obviously, we needed the knowledge of a concrete block plant expert. Who could be better than the owners we had talked with earlier? So we pressed them into service to make the trip to Guatemala to supervise all the planning we needed to do. Thus, one of the owners, another God's man, appeared on the scene—Ernie Kennedy. He put his block plant experience into practice, and we began to make ready to receive the plant. The first thing we needed was a sturdy concrete structure and platform where the block plant could be bolted and stabilized. We are talking block a plant here, and the measurements had to be precise because we did not have a crane at our disposal. It sounded like we had one shot at it, and that was it. When we finished setting the last big bolt, Ernie seemed to be happy. The next thing was to make sure that we had abundant water. A stream ran close to the property, and we were able to channel that for our use. The banks of sand were easy to find and highly accessible. We ordered the concrete for the cement, and it began to arrive. We had to build some provisional housing with a kitchen, and that's where my wife, Elaine, came in. We pitched a tent on the parcel of land, and that is where we lived. Don Salomon began the hiring process. Now, all we needed was the block plant and electricity! For some reason, the national electrical company was dragging its feet on the hookup, and we discovered that the hookup required a heavy-duty—an *extra* heavy-duty—transformer. We had to get moving to make contacts and find out where to get a hold of that kind of transformer. That was a whole other issue.

Finally, the day came when we heard the news that the concrete block plant had arrived and was ready to be unloaded at the dock in Santo Tomas. It would be quite a road trip to the port from where we were in Sacapulas, so we asked our pilot friend, Bill Overhulser, if he would be willing to fly down and see to it that the concrete block plant was loaded on a tractor trailer and then delivered to us upcountry. He replied that he would be glad to.

As we were thinking about the block plant being unloaded onto the platform, we realized that it had to be in a specific position on the flatbed in order to be unloaded properly. We had no crane, and according to Ernie we had only one chance to get it right. We relayed the information to Bill, but it did not get to him in time. The concrete block plant had already been loaded on the truck, but Bill felt that it was in the right position. A couple of days went by, and we heard that the block plant was heading up toward the capital. Authorities in the capital decided that the block plant had to be reloaded onto another flatbed in order to fit under the bridges to get to our area. So, it was reloaded and then rerouted; they were taking a route we did not recommend! We were in a dilemma. We were wondering what was happening.

You can imagine our anxious spirit when we heard, "Here comes the truck!" We gazed intensely as it slowly made the turn into our compound. Can you imagine our release when Ernie announced,

"You know what? It is on the right way!" I don't know how you feel about that, but I want to tell you that my Father is concerned about every detail (the drop of a miracle). It had been put on the wrong way at the dock, but because it had to be moved to a low-boy in the capital to fit under the bridges, it had been put on the right way for our unloading!

Now the challenge came to unload that block plant onto those bolts on that platform. The first thing we had to do was to get almost two thirds of the Land Rover buried on the other side of the platform. We peeled off the winch cable to connect it to the block plant. Ernie had the men place large pipes for the block plant to roll on as it was being pulled toward the bolts. My job was to coax the Land Rover to do its share of pulling while Ernie supervised the placing of the pipes. Okay, my heart began to beat a little faster. I connected the winch, cinched up the cable, and began to slowly pull the block plant. I could see that the whole chassis of the Land Rover was straining, but it was holding and the block plant was moving. Ernie kept those pipes rolling. Everyone was doing their part on cue. Now the commands were coming— "Slowly, now. Slowly. Only a few more inches to go. Okay, hold it!" I was praying big time because the winch was a little temperamental and didn't always stop when I wanted it to. But that day it obeyed. A few more nudges and Ernie announced that the plant was lined up perfectly with the bolts. With a few chocks and shims and jacks and some human effort, the pipes were removed and the block plant plopped down precisely where it was supposed to. Only Ernie could have made such precise measurements and maneuvering to make it happen so perfectly. Then it was bolted to its new home to begin a ministry.

Then, the process began to put more of the block plant parts together and wait for the electric hookup. We were getting close to the final assembly and needed juice. When we had come up with the transformer and had it delivered to our plant site, we thought that we were really ready to start. We had made various inquiries to the government office but gotten no results. We felt a little frustrated.

We had come so far, and now we lacked the integral component to make it work. We waited a few more days, and still no utility power trucks were in sight. I decided to put a little sacred politics to work. I had really hesitated to use the trump card, but I came to my wit's end. On a Saturday afternoon, I called a good friend in the town of Quetzaltenango. He owned a clothing factory and had such a bubbly, dynamic personality that he had many, many friends and contacts. It was worth a try. It was a small wonder that I even got him on the phone. But as the number was dialed in the telegraph room in Sacapulas, he picked up on the other end. We went through the various greetings, and then I got down to business. I told him of our dire need to have electricity in order to get the block plant into operation and that we had tried every avenue to no avail. He shared with me that it was an opportune moment because that very evening he was going to the opera with the director of the electric energy district in our area.

On Monday morning, the line crew was working on putting up the huge new transformer and hooking up the power lines to the plant. Now, we were on our way! Final assembly took place.

There were a lot of instructions and planning and teaching the new workers their various jobs. We put a high, strong emphasis on safety because this was the first time many had ever worked around heavy equipment. All of the materials were stockpiled and ready to go. We had a couple of trial runs, and it seemed that the machine was ready to be put into use. Obviously, with such a project there is always a little bit of fine tuning. We were so glad that Ernie was on the scene. Finally, the moment came for the final test, and we were all in great anticipation. The machine cranked up and made all of those noises that you would expect of a concrete block plant and some maybe that you wouldn't expect. We all huddled around the last stage where the block is finally pressed into its form. The press came down and back up again, and there in front of us was a magnificent cement block. We bowed our heads and lifted up a prayer of thanksgiving, but as we looked back we discovered that the block was disintegrating in front of us. So we went back to the drawing board and did more tweaking. Needless to say, that first block was a lesson in humility. But the day came when the press came down and the blocks came through as some of the best blocks ever made in Guatemala.

We then began distribution. The blocks flowed throughout our area, and through the years we were delighted to see many buildings standing because of a vision and our Father's touch of the drop of a miracle. All the praise goes to Him!

The provisional building where Ernie slept, I guess could be called a bedroom because the kitchen was outside along with the bathrooms. As you can imagine, we had a rather rustic environment. Ernie, standing over six feet tall, carried some trademarks on his forehead. The Guatemalans had built the provisional building and made it their size. It seemed that almost every time Ernie came through the bedroom door and the outside door, he banged his forehead on the door jamb. God bless Ernie. He never lost his sense of humor. On one occasion, he grabbed a paintbrush and created a signboard to hang over the doorway that read, "The Sacapulas Waldorf Astoria."

Our home church of Fork and Waugh Methodist wanted to help us rebuild a church in our area. The church that was close to where don Salomon lived had suffered a lot of damage in the earthquake, and the church people had decided to rebuild. We decided it would be a great opportunity for those churches in Maryland to participate, so a work team was put together. They came for two weeks and laid the walls with cement blocks from our plant, put on the roof, put in some windows, and then left some money to install a tile floor. It was a blessed experience for all. And I think it comes together with a statement of one of the men who came on the work team. On the last day we were all there, the church people in the town of Chicaman lined up on one side of the church building and we lined up on the other. We were going to say goodbye. We each crossed the room, embraced, and shook hands. One man, Robert, said that when he hugged and shook hands with the leader of the church, it was like he got a transfusion. I think we all could say the same thing. The embraces and the thankfulness of the people struck our lives and surged through our very beings. We certainly got more out of that experience than the people that we came to help—a drop of a miracle.

The day came when Ernie had to leave. And we knew, too, that there would be a day when we would have to leave and go on to other issues in the field. So we began to turn over the block plant and its operations to some very capable people. It didn't happen right away, but then we had to say goodbye to the concrete block plant and its operations. There also came a day when the block plant had done its part. The national conference decided that the plant had fulfilled its mission in our area and decided to sell it. What was so neat was that the Salvation Army bought it and moved it to another area of Guatemala, so it was still doing its sacred duty. We saw the block plant later in operation outside of a town about forty-five minutes from the capital. In fact, one time when Ernie came to visit us, we took him to see it, and it was almost like seeing an old friend.

CHAPTER 6

Pablo! Oh, Pablo! Where Are You?

At 3:20 a.m. on February 4, 1976, the world seemed to stop. Actually, the world shook rather violently for about thirty-three seconds before that time, the result of a 7.0-magnitude earthquake. Only those who have gone through the devastation, the stark fear, and the aftershocks of an earthquake can relate. It is not just the earthy stuff but the shock to life—what happens to the house you live in, churches, villages, towns, cities, and the nation—that sucks the life out of you. When the very thing that you walk on and build on and that you think is so stable begins to rock and roll and come apart, a part of you comes apart too.

Everyone I talk to, even to this day, knows exactly where they were when the world seemed to be coming apart. Some people have even dated other events from that date.

Elaine and I were in the capital city and were staying at the seminary. The wooden framed second floor rumbled and swayed so much that when I got out of bed, I couldn't stand up. Finally, the thirty-three seconds passed, and I was able to pull myself up to the window and look out. An eerie silence engulfed the city. Billows of dust and smoke rose slowly, tinted by fires and flashes of electric wires sputtering and flashing and withering as if in a death spasm as they snapped from their poles. It was a display and a morning that no one would soon forget.

The light of dawn found us all wondering just how bad it had been and how bad it was. We began to think of our children, who were away at boarding school. We began to think of our colleagues and the other towns and villages and how they had fared. And we began to think, *What do we do now? What are our next steps?*

Roads were closed. There was no power and communicating and networking with others was a challenge. What were we going to do?

Ah, in stepped the drop of a miracle! A Guatemalan friend offered his plane and pilot so we could survey the area. We flew over the school where the children were; there was not much damage. Everything looked okay. Then we flew over our towns in the north, and everything looked all right there too. We turned toward the villages to the south and toward the capital, and we were shocked to see what seemed like complete devastation, especially the village of Joyabaj, where our colleagues Bill and Rachel lived.

We decided to land and confirm our disbelief. Reality set in quickly as it looked even worse on the ground. We walked through the rubble and right by Bill and Rachel's house. When I finally got my bearings, it was as if the house did not exist—just a few jagged walls standing amid the rubble. And of all things, the president of our mission board, Cal Harvey, and his wife were staying with the Bill and Rachel. What joy filled my heart when I saw all four of them alive and well except for a few scratches.

They had experienced the drop of a miracle as they escaped falling roofs and walls. Bill and Cal became drops of a miracle as they rescued at least seven other people from the rubble. But that is another part of the story that they can tell best.

I could tell from the extent of the devastation that we needed to get some help to them as soon as possible. We made a quick trip to our town to pick up some items we thought that we would need. As soon as the townsfolk heard that we were heading back to Joyabaj, they showered us with things to take—clothes, food, tools, and other items. We did not have enough room for all of the stuff. Navigating the road with two big vats of cooked black beans was a real challenge. But, finally, we arrived back in Joyabaj.

The town had turned the soccer field into a staging area for the injured to be picked up by helicopter. We decided to park and camp there. The people of Joyabaj were still discovering the dead and bringing the injured to the soccer field, and the Chinook helicopters were still arriving and departing. When we saw those big US Chinooks come rumbling in it sure made us proud of the USA.

Translators were needed as the helicopters had US Army crew members and medical corps nurses on board. We were delighted to put our English and Spanish to work.

Injured people from the outlying villages began to trickle in. One day in the line of the injured was a boy about ten or eleven years old. The line moved quickly for the processing to board the helicopter. The young boy came up to Elaine and told her that he had severe pain in his hip and leg. She began writing on the clipboard. The next thing they knew, they were in front of the loading bay. The army corps nurse leaned out of the bay and asked, "What have you got there?"

"A young boy from a village with intense pain in his hip and leg," Elaine responded.

The nurse and Elaine asked and translated rapid-fire questions. "What is your name?" "What is your condition?" "Where do you live?"

With the quick translations, the quick answers, the quick decisions, the clicking of the other patients being strapped in, the notes on the clipboards, and the "We're loaded!" calls, the blades cranked up and began to whirl. Someone would yell, "Room for one more!" and the bay door became a blur. When the roar subsided and the dust settled, Pablo was gone.

He was headed to the capital to get immediate help. It was the right idea and the right decision—right?

Guess who showed up at the improvised airstrip a few hours later? Yep, Pablo's parents! Where they had been earlier, we didn't know.

"Where is our son?" they asked.

"He's gone—airlifted out to the hospital in the capital," we answered.

"Which one?" they asked.

"I am not sure," was the answer. With that, we could see the desperation creeping into their eyes and hear it in their voices. Desperation became full blown when we gave more vague answers about Pablo's destination and treatment.

I thought, *What's the problem? How hard could it be to locate Pablo in the city?* After all, there were not that many hospitals around. I tried to reassure the parents by saying that Elaine and I would make a special trip to find Pablo, and I added, with haste, that we would get word to them as soon as possible. The parents were grateful, but they made it rather clear that they were holding us responsible for their son. I understood their reasoning, and I also understood that I needed a drop of a miracle!

Early the next morning, we drove off on this accountability mission. We had no laptop and no tablet—just a clipboard accompanied us. We decided to start at the airport.

"Where did all the injured go?" we asked.

"They went to all the local hospitals, and when we say *all,* we mean all," we were told.

"Okay," I said to Elaine, "let's start at the major hospitals. I'm sure they must have some type of admissions record."

We left as the din of the airport, swarming with planes and helicopters, reminded us that it was still a very busy place. We had high hopes as we began the search.

We got to the first major hospital—no luck. At the second, no luck. "Do you remember seeing a young, ten- to eleven-year-old

Mayan boy with a bad hip, bad leg? Pablo is his name ?" That became the question and our cry.

We moved on to the smaller hospitals and were met with more of the same: "Sorry, don't remember seeing anyone like that." The days became a blur.

We were at the end of our searching file, and the clipboard stared back at us with a lot of scribbled and crossed-off names. There was one last stop. The medical staff people had been very helpful and had given us many ideas of where to keep looking. As we worked down the list, I believe they began to feel the cloud of desperation we were under. At this last name on the list, we got one more point of hope.

The head nurse had heard about the US Army putting up a tent hospital about forty-five minutes north of the capital just off the main road. So the next morning, we packed up and headed north. We began to reflect as we drove north. With so many patients, so many names, and so many faces, it just wasn't possible to remember everyone. Were we expecting too much? We knew this could be our last hope. *But wait,* we thought, *isn't our God the God of the impossible? Doesn't He delight sometimes to surprise us with the unveiling of mystery? How about that drop of a miracle?*

We rounded a curve, and there was the huge tent just off the road. When we entered the tent, we were greeted by the head nurse. We posed our usual question, and then we got the answer: "Well, do you know what? I do remember a boy with a bad leg." I am sure she could tell that a great sigh of relief flooded over us.

The nurse said that she remembered the young boy because she thought that his leg or hip was broken. She said, "He did seem to be in a lot of pain, and it was a concern for us. We ran some tests and then some x-rays. It was through the tests that we discovered that it was an old injury. It seems that his hip had been broken when he was younger." When the x-rays showed that there was no new injury, they presumed that, when the earthquake occurred, Pablo may have leaped out of bed or done some other maneuver that strained his hip and leg. Because he improved so dramatically, he was released because they needed the room. And, yes, they remembered his name.

But wait, released where?

There were other cases like Pablo's, so the government had set up a provisional orphanage just up the road, less than a half mile away.

I guess this must have been the first time Pablo had been out of his village. The earthquake, the helicopter ride, the different faces and language likely had him somewhat disoriented. At the hospital, he couldn't come up with the name of his village, so he was put up in the orphanage in the hopes that someone would come looking for him. We did not waste any time in getting to the car and heading that half mile up the road.

We were greeted at the front desk, and once again we stated our business and held our breath. The young woman scanned her list.

"Why, yes, there is a Pablo here!" she said. "And I think he is outside playing with the other children."

On Pablo's eleventh day away from home, we found him. It seems a little strange, but even though we had only seen Pablo for those few moments days earlier, as soon as we saw him with the other children we knew exactly who he was. There was no need to wait to make any kind of positive identification. "That's Pablo!" we said.

We signed some paperwork, put Pablo in the car, and paused to praise our Father for the drop of a miracle. What a joyous ride it was back toward the state capital of Quiche.

The pilot who owned his own plane and had helped us with the concrete block plant was living in Quiche. Bill Overhulser had been flying for us a few years and then had gone back to the States. He had returned to Guatemala before the earthquake under the Lord's direction. (Now that is a whole other story.) He became a great blessing right after the earthquake, flying many, many mercy missions. I was hoping I would find him at home; I had another mercy mission for him.

We arrived at Bill's house, and he was home. I shared with him Pablo's story. "Would you be willing to fly him home?" I asked.

"Sure," Bill said. "I'd be delighted to. Let's get to the airstrip and get the plane cranked up."

I think Pablo's parents had been camping out at the Joyabaj "airstrip" because we had no trouble finding them. Can you imagine the reunion?

Can you imagine our relief, our sheer joy, and our deep, heartfelt praise?

I still have that picture burned in my memory—mother, father, and son, arm in arm, hand in hand, walking off into a spectacular sunset.

They say that the earthquake destroyed close to a million houses. But it didn't (couldn't!) destroy those people's homes. We saw how quickly the families gathered, and once they were together, even in the poorest, most improvised shelters, they were home. Some of the stories are thrilling, detailing how people journeyed over almost insurmountable obstacles to reach home. Pablo's story is just one of many.

We sometimes wonder if Pablo thinks about his experience. We sure do! We think about how quickly everything can change. In fact, in a matter of seconds, everything can change. So think about real security, that "I hold you in My hand and no one can pluck you out!" kind of security. That is an unshakable promise.

We find ourselves thinking that there are a lot of Pablos out there who are away from home. We are reminded that we do not know what a day will bring, so we need to bring to every new day our efforts guided by the Holy Spirit to do our best to get everyone home.

I can always remember the day I came home! I hope you can too. If you can't, I know Someone is looking for you. And I know He will go to unbelievable lengths to find you.

Pablo! Oh, Pablo! Where are you? We wait in anticipation for that drop of a miracle!

CHAPTER 7

Side Track

I would like to take a moment for a little sidetrack here. One of the truck drivers we hired for the concrete block plant project drove one of our trucks off the road one night. He crashed right through the rock wall of a guardrail, down over a high bank, and to the edge of the river. The truck came to rest right side up in the sand. The next morning my son, Don, and I went to survey the damage. Where the truck was resting, the high bank and the river impeded any type of a recovery at that point. I started up the truck, and it ran. It seemed there was no damage to the engine, and as I looked across the river it seemed to me that there was a way out. Where the truck had landed, the river hugged the bank and there was no way to drive down on that side of the river. The river made a lazy U a little farther down and formed a kind of island on the opposite side of the river in front of us. If I could get the truck through the river and to the other side where the island was, I could then make a run from the island, through the river again, and to the other side to the road. The high bank along the river tapered down and seemed to be low enough where I could actually drive the truck back up on the road. It was worth a try. Don and I discussed the strategy.

First, I felt I needed to bend out the fender, which had been crushed in on the front tire when the truck went through the stone wall. I retrieved a huge crowbar from the block plant compound and went to work. I wedged the bar in and began to pry. I was making headway; there's nothing like the fulcrum principle—pry, pry, and pop, pop, and pop! The fender was free, but it seemed something else had popped too. I peered under the open hood and into the engine, where I discovered that I had somehow hooked the crowbar onto the fuel pump and gas line and had broken the fuel pump off. Oh, no! But you know, where there is a will, there is a way—and in this case the way was gravity. I could put Don on the truck cab's roof holding a gas can, and I could run a plastic hose from the can to the carburetor. Whoopee! Instant fueling system. We did a dry run without trying to move the truck, and it started and seemed to run well. Now for the real deal and the first run across the river to the island. "Hold tight, Don!" I called out. "Here we go!" I revved the engine, and *splash*! We plowed into the river and across we went, arriving on the dry land of the island. Well, well, the first step of our salvage operation was a success; now for the second stage. We regrouped, I made sure Don was okay, and I took a deep breath mingled with prayer. "Okay, Don," I called out again, "here we go again. Hold tight!" Everything seemed to be running well until we were about halfway across and made an extra big splash. In fact, water was running into the cab. I didn't realize that it was that deep. The engine sputtered, coughed, and died, flooded out, with us in the middle of the river. Don abandoned the top of the cab, I pushed the door open against the water, and we waded (almost had to swim) to the road. I looked at the truck and at the black clouds brewing west of the river. I thought, *What do we do now? If the rains come, our truck will be washed away.*

We got out on the road, and what do you know? There was a bus going to our town of Nebaj. I flagged down the driver and asked him to bring me a huge chain that I had in my garage on his return trip in the morning. I told him to give a note I had written to Elaine and to ask her where the chain was in my garage. (In the note I tried to tell Elaine where I thought the chain was, hoping she could find it!) The next morning, they showed up with the chain. One of the members of our church in Nebaj was working with the electric company in Sacapulas, and he came driving their big tractor that they used to haul the huge concrete posts for the electric lines. He was delighted that he could help. He backed the tractor up into the river, we hooked the big chain to the truck, and out of the river the truck came. The rain had held off. The truck had to be towed to the town hall, where it was to be impounded until an investigation could be conducted to determine what had caused the accident. They also needed to investigate whether they needed to levy any fines on the driver.

The truck sat there at the town hall for months, and all the while, we kept borrowing parts off it for the other trucks. When it finally came time to give an account to the government about our equipment, we were hard pressed to present any details. The wheels, the tires, the cab, the transmission, and the motor were all gone. It looked like a skeleton that had been picked clean. The bare-boned chassis was all that remained. We could not even find the serial numbers.

As for my son Don, the whole experience seemed to have left quite an impression. How he held onto the gas can and the plastic hose while balancing his own body on that cab roof of the truck I'll never know. When we plowed through the rock-strewn river, it must have been quite a ride—one he has never forgotten. Yes, he made that first step into manhood. It was his rite of passage.

Blessed are the parents who can be there for the rites of passage in their children's lives. Obviously, those moments are filled with excitement and drama. But we all know that parenting is also filled with a ton of the mundane during the day-to-day journey. I have discovered that it is easy to get into the mode of being too busy and neglecting being present. Even in the sense of doing the "good work," we forget and leave behind the best—those moments when we would have had the windows of teachable moments, when children are so tender and open, when they are sensitive to the charged atmosphere so filled with spiritual components. It's a small wonder that Jesus used parables, those earthy teachings with heavenly meanings.

I have discovered that there is a priestly function in repairing my son's bicycle. I have found that there is a sacredness in playing with my daughter as she made papier-mache ice cream in the patio. There was a holy aura over the sandbox I made for my young son. He used it to write out letters and words to help his learning process. I could fill a few more pages; I wish I could fill a book! With all of those priestly duty moments, I wish I could have captured more.

Don't *you* let them slip by!

And while I am at it, let me get a little preachy here. You don't have to wait for some special day to give them some special gifts.

- Give the gift of time. Play with them with eternity in perspective.
- Give them the gift of surprise, the amazement of the divine splendor that surrounds us every day.
- Give them the gift of security. In this age of cynicism and compounded social and moral problems, they need a hug of love and refuge.
- Give them the gift of self-esteem. Reassure them that they are made in God's image. Remind them of who they are and to whom they belong. Christ Jesus died for them.
- Give them the gift of joy—peace dancing. Smother them with the joy of the Lord, which is your strength.
- Give them the gift of accountability. Sure, they have rights and privileges, but their greatest right is to give up their rights for others. It is a blessing to grasp the attitude of servanthood.
- Give them the gift of believable parents. Be honest, full of integrity, and free of pretense. Be full of earthy humanness and forgiveness.
- And don't forget that love is the greatest gift. It never fails!

May you have the greatest privilege on earth! And, yes, you can take it with you!

CHAPTER 8

Eleven Strong Men in the Early Morning Sun

Some of my colleagues will be thinking that I am going to write about the Baltimore Colts (oops, I mean the Baltimore Ravens—I have really dated myself!) and an early-morning practice session. No, I am going to write about something much more important and exciting.

We heard news about a sick Ixil woman in a village about seven hours from where we lived. Reports had been sent to our town by two men who had visited her home. Miguel and Diego, two of the church leaders in a village somewhat close to the Ixil woman's home had heard about her too, so they took time out of their corn-planting schedule to go and visit her and her husband. They discovered a very sick woman. They reported later that they had never seen someone's stomach swollen as large as hers. Miguel and Diego marveled that she was still alive. These two were, however, coming from another perspective. With their spiritual sensitivity, they sensed that Nan El had more than a physical need. Miguel and Diego then spent the rest of the afternoon sharing the power of Jesus to save and heal, and Nan El and her husband listened and came under great conviction.

Then, that very afternoon, Nan El, out of her great spiritual need, put her faith in Jesus. Lying on that plank bed, so desperately ill, she said, "Whether I get better or not is not the issue anymore. What really matters is what has happened to me now. I now have Jesus in my heart!"

Miguel and Diego had another agenda. They explained to Nan El and her husband that there was a hospital available for her, but in her condition, the hospital may as well have been on the other side of the world. How could she possibly get there? Her stomach was so ballooned that she couldn't get out of bed, let alone walk. "Wait," the men said. "We have a way. We can carry you out of here to town. We also know someone in town who will take you to the hospital."

So Miquel and Diego sent word to me in town of their plan. I sent a message back: "Just get her to where the road ends, and I will be waiting with the Land Rover to pick you all up." The news also got out to the other villages. When some of the other believers got the word, they quickly volunteered to help. They set a date for the carryout and the rendezvous.

At 2:00 a.m. on the designated day, nine men along with Miguel and Diego showed up at Nan El's home—eleven strong men in the early morning hours ready to serve. They had a makeshift chair/stretcher lashed to a tumpline, and each man took a turn carrying this precious cargo.

The sun was just coming up as I rounded the last bend where the road ended. The early morning rays filtered through the trees, and a light mist of holy aura encompassed the group. What a sight: eleven strong men in the early morning sun—a shining spectrum of the drop of a miracle! Wow, you talk about a sunrise service!

We had the privilege to take that precious cargo, Nan El, on to the hospital. Her faith in Jesus never wavered and was a constant reminder to those at the hospital: "Whether I get better or not," she said, "the most important thing has already happened to me. I now have Jesus's healing in my heart and life." It was a deep perception that Nan El referred to the spiritual experience as a healing. Little did she know she was about to receive another healing.

We never did find out what her medical diagnosis was. I am not sure we could ever find out. Whatever it was, it began to shrink away. Her stomach began to shrink down and down and down. She got her appetite back. She got her strength back, and she was able to walk. Finally, she was released from the hospital and returned home. Actually, she walked the last four hours from the bend in the road where it ends, at the spot of the early morning encounter weeks before.

A few months after Nan El returned home, we had a baptismal service close to where she lived (four hours away). I'll never forget the scene. We were all gathering to begin the service when I glanced up and thought I saw a mirage. Coming across the field of knee-deep grass that they used for their thatched roofs was Nan El! Walking tall and straight, she came down the trail in what seemed like a dream. She had heard about the ceremony, and she came to be baptized. And baptize we did! It was a holy moment when she stepped into the stream. There was a hushed sacredness when she went under the water. There seemed to be a roll of jubilation and applause when she surfaced and stepped out of the stream. Only God can create these moments. The drops of a miracle came cascading down, reminding us of forgiveness, redeeming, cleansing, healing, identifying, rejoicing, and on and on. Oh, God is good!

Isn't it wonderful that the Father gives us an opportunity to play a role in the advancement of His kingdom? Two men took time out of their schedules to journey to Nan El's home. They did not know what kind of a response they were going to get, but they went. They shared what they had, and then they left the rest to God.

And guess what? Nan El responded, believed, and put her faith and hope in Jesus as her Savior. They offered to carry her to the hospital, and nine other men responded to help. Their visit did not end. They had a mutual concern that was put into action, and they did whatever was needed. There was an almost unbelievable spin-off from their obedience to God's Word.

As I think about this story, it reminds me to check my priorities. How willing am I to commit to and obey what God is saying? And am I willing to ultimately leave the results to God and trust for a drop of a miracle?

CHAPTER 9

The Pursuit of Palop

It seemed like an apparition. There in the misty twilight stood a Mayan Quiche man. I think he was about as surprised as the Ixil evangelist Jose and I were. We greeted each other and began a conversation. We discovered that Vicente Hernandez lived in the village of Palop on the western slope of Ixil country. It was a small village that was nestled in the mountain range that marks the end of the Ixil speaking area.

We were both about a day and a half's walk from home. Jose and I had been traveling in the area of the coffee plantations, La Estrella and Cobadonga, in the northeast of Ixil country. Vicente was on his journey to check on his corn crop. Where he lived in Palop had its challenges for growing corn because of the altitude and steep rocky terrain. Fortunately, he was able to find someone who was willing to negotiate for some planting sites on the other side of the coffee plantation, La Perla (the pearl). We began to think, and I said to him, "It sure seems like a long walk to your cornfield." He said, "Well, you know that down at this altitude, I am able to harvest two crops of corn and beans a year, and it is well worth the trips."

He was a little curious, too, about why we were so far from our home. We were able to share with him the reason that we were on the trail and connect it to planting and harvesting. We said we were sowing the good word of Jesus and that it was well worth the trip too. We had the wonderful privilege to see lives changed. Jose could speak Quiche, and what an asset that was. Vicente seemed to be interested and said perhaps we could visit him some day in Palop. We gave him some literature and expressed our desire to visit him some day. Then I guess we put that future trip on the back burner.

One day, Jose and I were traveling to visit some of the congregations and villages in the western area of Ixil country. We stopped one day on that trip on a small bridge to rest. Well, guess who was coming up on the small bridge to rest too? It was Vicente! He was coming back from his cornfields. We greeted one another heartily and talked again of our visit to his home. This time, we could sense urgency as he spoke with us. His oldest son was sick, and he said he had other things to discuss with us. So right then and there, we set a date for our visit—July 6.

The days passed quickly, and soon Jose and I were preparing for our visit to Palop. It was about a ten-hour trip. Some hours into the trip on the trail, I remarked to Jose, "I wonder if Vicente will be waiting for us?" I could tell from Jose's remark that he was a little anxious too: "Yes," he said, "I sort of wonder too. Maybe he is off to his cornfield."

About three hours outside of Palop, we met a young man with an *azadon* (hoe) over his shoulder who told us that Vicente was waiting for us. Our anxiety lifted. When we reached the crest of the next hill, there was Vicente, smiling and holding a jug of cold coffee for us. As we traveled on together, we discussed Jesus. The next thing we knew, we were in Vicente's front yard.

We continued on the topic of Jesus. We discovered quickly that Vicente was hungry and thirsty for spiritual food and drink. Late that evening, we had the privilege of helping Vicente with the personal decision to put his faith in Jesus Christ based upon the scriptures—the Holy Word. We had the delightful privilege to see Vicente respond with great affirmation.

"You know," Vicente said, "I've been studying these things for three years, and now I understand. I believe in Jesus!" And we believed that Vicente experienced the forgiveness of his sins and the new birth, right then and there!

This isn't the end of the story. Six other men from Palop were in that meeting that night, and we know that the Holy Spirit was talking to them that night, too. Jose returned to the village and began to teach and share with Vicente and his family. Little by little, the whole village was beginning to be affected and influenced by the good news of Jesus. We were so glad that we took that visit to Palop off the back burner and made a rather simplistic but firm decision that day on the bridge.

God our Father can take the simplest decision and turn it into a turning point in history. Am I making too much of this? I don't think so. Chase down some of what you might think of as just very simple decisions, not earthmoving or earthshaking. But, wow! How they turned out to be game changers! And what about "for the want of a nail the shoe was lost"? A simplistic decision to shoe the horse could have changed history. Ask the people in Palop about a simple decision on the bridge. Take decisions off the back burner and offer them up to the Father, and then watch the results flow—those drops of a miracle. Sometimes we toss and turn and fret about God's will for us, but could it be that God's will is for us is to make a decision?

Sometimes, along with some of those decisions, comes a little discomfort. I shall always remember that night in Palop because it was the coldest night I ever spent in Guatemala. After the late night of sharing was over, I rolled out my sleeping bag. I was as close to the fire in the three stones area, which served as the cooking stove. I felt assured that warmth coming off the fire and the stones would radiate sufficiently to keep me comfortable all night, but I awakened at about two o'clock in the morning wondering why I felt a chill and stuck my head out of the sleeping bag to discover that the fire, for all practical purposes, was out. I stuck my head back in and hoped for the best. It did not happen. Not just a chill now, but cold, high mountain cold began creeping up from the bottom of my sleeping bag. I began to curl up my legs and knees until I was as rolled into as tight of a self- hugging ball as I could possibly be. It did not help. The cold dirt floor added to the advantage that the cold had over me and my bag. We were no match. Cold had won and chilled me to the marrow of my bones. I had no choice but to give up. I abandoned the sleeping bag. I already had on all the clothes that I had brought with me, so I thought that maybe going outside would offer a chance to get a little circulation going. Once outside the door, I found it was just as cold as inside. *Oh, well,* I thought, *at least I'm not bound up in the freezing cocoon.* Movement helped some, but I found myself longing for the dawn. *Where is that sun?* I guess some of my companions that night probably thought, *What a spiritual guy, up so early in the morning.* If only they would have known! I had been in Alaska during my Navy Seabee experience. We even had Arctic survival training and would play freeze out, but I never felt as cold there as I did that night in Guatemala. Sometimes when I have a freezing experience, I reflect on that night. I realize that no matter how bad it gets, if you hang in there, the sun does come up!

CHAPTER 10

To Ilom and Beyond

How do you open up a village? How do you go about getting the opportunity to present the good news about Jesus? How do you go about not just opening and presenting but actually penetrating the village and planting a church? You don't want to just go skipping through the plaza and announcing, "Boy, have we got great news for you!" You want to be involved in something much more permanent.

So, my colleague Gale Morris and I began to think about such a village. One village called Ilom began to come into focus. We had been hearing reports that there was no solid witness for Jesus and that the village was rather unique in the sense that it was surrounded by a huge coffee plantation and had a history of deep culture heritage. There had been rumors that the conquistadores had hidden some treasure on some of the lower downhill slopes of the village. Various digs had been conducted throughout the years but had no success (as far as we know). Despite this flurry of outside activity and the pressures of the coffee plantation, the village had held to its traditional ways. The impressions we heard of the village were intriguing, exciting, and challenging. Ilom was about a day and a half's walk from our town.

Nebaj was the gateway to Ixil country. Out of Nebaj, we could travel north, northeast, or northwest and hit all of the main roads and trails that led to all the towns and villages in Ixil country. The main road that led to Chajul and Cotzal came right through Nebaj. Traveling out of Nebaj was mostly downhill as all the trails and roads dropped in elevation down to Ixcan and the Zona Reina.

So when traveling to Ilom, we went down. Now I don't mean straight down but a gentle, sloping down. It was an easy down; it was coming back to Nebaj that was a little tougher.

There were two trails out of Nebaj to Ilom, and they followed the heavily wooded, steep, mountainous ravine of the main river that flowed toward the Ixcan and Zona Reina area. One trail was on the eastern side of the river gorge, went through a lot of small villages, and linked up with a trail in the village of Juil. The trail in Juil went down (and this was a *down*!) the mountainside to the river and over the bridge to the coffee plantations. The other trail leaving Juil went to the east to Chajul. During the coffee harvest, the coffee plantations used this trail to transport their coffee with pack mules to Chajul, which was a staging area for loading the trucks.

The other trail was on the western side of the mountainous ravine and traveled along and somewhat below the ridge. It was the trail less traveled, and there were only scattered inhabitants along the path. Sometimes we could travel all day and not meet anyone else. This was the trail we were later to choose.

The reinforcement of our thoughts came with nudges from the Holy Spirit. We began to pray. Then we began to pray in earnest. We decide to set aside a month to fast and pray specifically for our venture to Ilom. You plan, you pray, and then the day comes to put feet to those plans. You step out.

But wait—other preparations are needed before that stepping-out day. In our case, we needed some horses to help carry some of the equipment. We needed food. We took in a lot of advice regarding which trails to take, where to stay overnight, and how if we started early on the first day, we might make the trip in one day.

We started the first day at 3:00 a.m., fully equipped and loaded. Saddles were cinched, a machete was slung over the saddle horn, and my trusty hunting knife was sheathed and attached to my belt. We had sleeping bags tied to back of the saddles, and food and other items filled the saddlebags. We were prepared to not just ride but to walk too.

We were blessed with a beautiful day to travel as we ventured out on that trail less traveled. You would have had to travel those trails in those days to appreciate the beauty and the pristine atmosphere, with the gorgeous wildflowers; the sparkling clear, cool streams that we could drink from, the silence, and the scarce traffic. We met only two fellow travelers that day, and they were going the opposite way. We plodded along with no urgency, captured by this seemingly other world. Even though there was a unique silence, the birds were still singing away, and we could still hear the distant, melodious roar of the water below. We became aware, also, of how the day had slipped by. The sun was beginning to drop behind the mountain range, and the next thing we knew darkness had engulfed us. We had forgotten how quickly it gets dark when the sun disappears behind the range. We had also forgotten how dark it can be when there is no other light except the stars. We began to think about where we were going to bed down because we knew we were still some distance from Ilom.

We were still negotiating the trail with our flashlights when we came upon a rather large tree that had fallen across the trail. We decided to get everything across the tree and then bed down. Gale's horse was in the lead, and we thought we would get him across first and then mine would follow. I tied a rope from Gale's horse to my saddle horn. Gale got on the other side of the log and began to coax his horse over the log. The horse made a great effort; he reared up and got his front feet across the log, but with the next lunge he did not get his rear legs up far enough to clear it. What happened next happened very, very fast. He began to slide down along the log on the downhill side. The rope on my saddle horn sprang taut. In a split second, I knew he was going to pull my horse and possibly me over the side of the steep ravine. I whipped out my hunting knife, and with one frantic slash I sliced the rope. And then, he was gone, tumbling and thrashing and making an unearthly noise as he rolled down the steep gorge. We quickly lost sight of him in the darkness and could only stand there in awe of all the noise we heard. Then, all of a sudden, we heard an abrupt, loud thud and what sounded like the deepest grunt and groan I have ever heard. Then there was silence. It was so dark that we could not see each other's expressions. I could only imagine what mine looked like—a completely dumbfounded, what-in-the-world-just-happened look of disbelief. We knew we had to get down there and see what happened. At first, I thought that the good news was that he had not gone all the way down to the river; we didn't hear any splashes.

When we scrambled down the steep slope with our flashlights, we came upon a scene that was hard to imagine. The horse was completely upside down with his feet sticking up into the air and the saddle still on his back—stuck under a huge log! His eyes were bigger than ever, and they seemed to reflect the flashlight beams with a combination of despair and disbelief. It took us a few moments to take in the situation. *How in the world did he ever get into this predicament, and how in the world are we ever going to get him out of it?*

We came up with an idea: could we possibly dislodge him from this wedged position by pushing and pulling? There was room under the log for someone to get on the other underside of the log and push. There was a hope that one of us could pull on his front legs and that would help. We were also counting on the horse to do his part. We thought that when he began to feel like he was getting just a little bit dislodged, he would, by instinct, make a great effort on his part for self-preservation. Granted, we were fully aware of the herculean task ahead of us. But what else could we do for this horse pinned under the log? Gale went below and began to push. I began to talk to the horse as I grabbed a front leg and started to pull. It seemed that the horse knew we were there to help, and he cooperated. Gale gave him just enough of a push to get him activated, and he began to squirm and wiggle. I guess he could feel himself getting a little freer because he was really putting in an effort to get out of there. He got to moving his front legs so frantically that I had to let go. Then there was more thrashing and grunting, and the next thing I knew he was on his feet. Believe me—it was a glorious moment!

The horse was a little shaky and twitched a few times. We checked him out with our flashlights, and he seemed okay. We zigzagged back up the steep incline and found my horse patiently waiting. We then decided to circumvent the tree in the path by going higher up the mountain and making our own trail. It was quite an effort, but we finally made our way up and then back down to the trail. Finally, we were able to make camp.

We awakened to a new day, and what a difference the bright sunshine made on our surroundings. We felt renewed and saddled up. Once again, we were on the trail and enjoying the trip when we came upon a fork in the trail. Both paths seemed to be worn the same amount. *Hmm, which one do we take?* we wondered. Just then, we heard what sounded like hoofbeats. And sure enough, a rider came into view. We had a traveling companion.

"Howdy," we said in greeting. We made some introductions. We came to find out that the rider was a schoolteacher and was headed for his school in Ilom. His arrival could not have been more providential (a drop of a miracle!) Not only was he going to get us on the right path, he threw in a bonus. He offered us the schoolhouse for our introduction into Ilom. What hospitality! He rode off with a wave and an "*Hasta la vista.*"

Later that afternoon, we arrived in Ilom, where we found the one-room schoolhouse and the teacher. He welcomed us and helped us find people to take care of our horses and a place to eat. We had some time before the sun went down, so we took a quick tour of the village before going back to the schoolhouse and unrolling our sleeping bags.

The next day we tried to get more acquainted with the village. At first, it looks like a typical Ixil village. We discovered that the inhabitants were a little more diverse as we heard a few different languages in the air. We used some of our Ixil and discovered that they spoke the Chajul Ixil dialect. They could understand us, but because of some differences, they knew right away we were not Chajul speakers. We stayed another day, picked up a few phrases, and met some more people. They seemed to be interested in our message. We thanked the schoolteacher for his hospitality, and he replied that the school would be open for us to use when we returned. We assured him that we would be back and asked him to pass the word.

We traveled back to Nebaj without any incident, and the horses did great. Thus, began the opening of Ilom and a series of many trips and blessed adventures.

CHAPTER 11

Back to Ilom

Our return trip to the village of the Ilom was postponed two times. When we finally set off, we decided that on the way, we would visit a coffee plantation known as La Perla. When we arrived at La Perla on Saturday, they were having a mini market day. We were able to take advantage of our time there by selling a few Bibles and sharing the good news about Jesus in the small plaza. We visited a few homes and bedded down for the night in one of the warehouses.

Early Sunday morning, with an exceptionally bright, clear blue sky, we left La Perla and made it to Ilom two hours later. Again, the one-room schoolhouse was open to us, and we spent that afternoon in anticipation of the coming night's service. This time, we were equipped with a supply of recently translated Bible stories about creation, the fall of man, and the coming of Jesus. Pap Lap, a new Ixil believer who was Ray Elliott's language informant and my part-time informant, was my companion on this trip. He was primed for teaching and preaching these lessons. I had also brought my dental instruments with me, so that afternoon I began to extract teeth and continued well into the evening by means of a flashlight and candles. Then, over a supper of black beans and eggs, we discussed the anticipated service. We all thought that the spectators to the tooth extractions and the actual patients would be gone and that perhaps only a few people would give us a hearing this night.

When we returned, we were delighted to see that no one had left. Everyone was waiting! We quickly surveyed the group and found only one or two who spoke only Spanish in the room, so we decided to keep everything in the Ixil language right from the start. We sang a few Ixil hymns and choruses, and one fellow right next to me almost snatched the small hymn book out of my hands. Then, Pap Lap began; he opened his small, mimeographed Bible storybook and began to read. Meanwhile, we handed out more copies in the candlelight to those who could read so that they could follow along. After every sentence, Pap Lap would stop reading, back up, and explain all that had been read and what he had said before. Pap Lap got all the way up through the fall of man before he thought he should stop. He then gave his own testimony.

Pap Lap shared that he had heard the good news about Jesus in Ixil for the first time a few years earlier. He said he had tried to shrug off the message, but some of his fellow Ixil companions who had put their faith in Jesus kept sharing Jesus with him. Finally, after reading some of the Gospel of Mark in Ixil, he became convinced that Jesus is who He said He is. Pap Lap knew and practiced all of the customs and rituals of the Ixil traditional religion, and he even practiced some of the Catholic rites to keep his account straight. Then one day, he was overcome with the love of God the Father. He made his decision for Jesus. He was overwhelmed with the sense of duty and obligation and privilege to share this good news with his fellow country people. He carried the credentials of a born-again Maya Ixil. The group of about thirty sat in rapt attention.

One-cent candles were still scattered throughout the one-room schoolhouse, after we unofficially closed the service. In that flickering light, those who had listened intently to the good news about Jesus Christ and His ability to forgive seemed to just hang around. Two men were very impressed with what was going on. In fact, they wanted to buy a copy of the Gospel of Mark in Ixil and a new, simplified version of the Spanish New Testament. They had a young Ixil man with them. They said that he could read, and they called him their *maestro* (teacher). The two men said that he would read to them and they would listen and think about all the stories; if it was the truth, they said they would certainly take it into consideration (and I thought, *Along with all of their other "stories"*). "So, Holy Spirit," I breathed out, "this is where You are going to have to do Your work!" They wanted more stories, and we promised we would bring some next time.

We wondered about these men as they went off into the dark. Had they been sent by the Mayan Ixil religious leaders to find out what we were up to? Were they genuinely interested? Could that young Ixil man read well enough in his heart language to communicate with understanding? And in the instance of Spanish, was he able to translate well enough? We prayed for them, and we wondered, waiting for a drop of a miracle.

CHAPTER 12

The Continued Quest for Ilom

We made plans to visit Ilom again, but this time, we made elaborate plans. A real project went into motion. We had to line up horses or mules to carry our equipment. The biggest challenges were the light plant and the movie projector. (I told you we had big plans!) The light plant was a generator that had a Briggs & Stratton gasoline engine bolted to it. The Briggs & Stratton motor supplied the power to run the generator. The gasoline engine presented its challenges as it could be temperamental at times. Most of the time we were up to the challenge. Transporting the light plant was a minor issue because we thought that we could rig it on an *aparjo* (saddle-like carrier) that we could cinch to a horse or mule. The projector was another issue. It was more cumbersome. We made a box to cover and protect it, but that made it heavier and bigger. However, we found someone who was willing to carry it. There was a special group of people who were like the Sherpas of Nepal, and their profession was to carry cargo. They were a special breed. The young man we hired had a worn, bald spot on his forehead where the *mecapal* (tumpline—a leather head strap with rope) rode. He had his own tumpline, and man, could he push and pull cargo. Most of his trips involved sacks of coffee, beans, and corn. He was way beyond the point of ever finding shoes to fit his humongous, wide feet. We packed some dental instruments and some medicine in our cargo rolls, and they were no problem.

So we had company on this trip, and with some expert traveling companions, we moved right along. Especially impressive was the young man carrying the projector box. He just trod along talking, laughing, and telling jokes while we panted to catch our breath and keep up.

We arrived in the village and showed a film about Jesus in the small plaza in front of the schoolhouse. I extracted a few pain-causing teeth and we were able to give out some medicine, all while sharing that it was in the name and love of Jesus. We had some moments sharing the good news in the schoolhouse and in some of the homes. We were using the book of Mark in Nebaj Ixil, and people perked up when we spoke Ixil. Some of the townspeople began to show interest in the Word.

As we prepared to leave the village, some of the people encouraged us to come back and even asked us to give them a date when we would return. One elderly Ixil man came up to me and said, "I can't read, but my grandson can. Leave me one of your Mark books, and I will have him read it to me. And if it is the truth, I'll believe!" I was delighted to hand him a book of Mark's Gospel, and my heart leaped because I knew what was going to happen. He was going to believe—because it is the truth!

One other man, though, sort of left me with a haunting thought. I thanked the townspeople for their hospitality and shouted, "Remember, God loves you!" Then out of the crowd, a man shouted back, "Oh, yeah, show me!" We returned to Nebaj with, "Oh, yeah, show me!" echoing in our heads.

Little did we realize that, as we planned our next trip to Ilom, we were in for an unexpected surprise. The Father smiled down upon us and said, "Let's give them a treat of an airplane ride!" Just think of a sixteen-hour walk cut to twenty to twenty-five minutes.

What a blessing it was. Bill Overhulser appeared out of the wild blue yonder with his helio-courier. His unique plane could land and take off on the distance of a football field. His coming to Guatemala was a drop of a miracle.

There was a semblance of an airstrip at the base of the mountainside where Ilom was nestled. It was owned by the coffee plantation. We began to ask around about using the airstrip and got permission.

What a great first ride to Ilom via the helio-courier! I spent most of the trip looking down at the trail that wound through the river valley. And then before I knew it, we were on the ground.

We took some ministry items—the light plant, projector, medicine, dental instruments, and some Bibles. And on this trip, my wife, Elaine, and our six-year-old son, Paul, came with us. A group from the village came to the airstrip to meet us, and they quickly packed up the cargo, hoisted the items onto their backs, and went up the mountain with us. When we arrived in the village, one of the men encouraged us to stay at his house and show the films, so we set up shop in his front yard and patio. This time, included in the cargo were the Jesus films and some other film from the US embassy, one of which was about the moon landing. We spread a sheet between two big pine trees, and that made it possible to be able to see the film on both sides of the sheet. We drew a crowd. I wondered where everyone was coming from. I also wondered what kind of word had gotten out about us. I could hardly imagine.

Elaine put the medicine to use right away. She discovered that the medicine for parasite worms really worked. The morning after getting the treatment, kids were bragging about how many worms they had passed. It almost sounded like a contest. In the front yard, we shared the gospel and extracted some teeth. There seemed to be more interest in the village about the good news of Jesus this time. Some of the men were still processing the message. We were also processing our plans and preparations and trusting to be open to the ministry of the Holy Spirit. We returned home with great expectations for the future of Ilom.

We made more trips to Ilom over time, and some great side moments occurred that made things interesting and kept us on our toes. Some moments awakened us to the reality of the spiritual battle in which we were engaged.

One day, I was preaching behind a makeshift pulpit in the front yard of one of the Ixil families' homes, a turkey came flying in. This was not one of those ground run things where the poor turkey tries to get off the ground. No, this was a full-flight maneuver. He came buzzing in over the thatched roof with landing gear down. His target was the pulpit, and he came in with wings a'flapping and feathers flying. Even though I was at the best point of my sermon, I thought that in the interest of common decency, I should abandon my position and get out of the way. Those turkeys, even though they were "domesticated," have to do a lot of scratching to eke out a living. So, fly they can—talk about open range! One person commented that the turkey got a lot more attention than I did, and it was said that he even woke a few people up. It is difficult to soar with eagles when you've been grounded by a turkey!

Another time I had the privilege of sharing the good news in the one-room schoolhouse. The room was filled to capacity with men and boys and a few women. My time to share came at the end of the service, and we were always anticipating a work of the Holy Spirit. I was getting close to the end of the message when I noticed movement and a scuffle of feet and bodies. There was a ripple effect on the back two rows. I first thought that it was a spiritual affect and an awakening. Then all of a sudden, the subtle movements became chaos. Men and women and boys scattered. The only thing was that there was only one door and two small windows. We had never thought of an exit plan. Nevertheless, a stampede ensued. Some who could fit went out the windows while the rest made a rush for the door. I happened to be standing close to the door and found it very difficult not to get evicted with the crowd. When the room cleared, we saw what the culprit was. It seems a snake had come into the room earlier and had escaped detection. It had curled up in a corner but then decided to make a move and slithered out across the floor! It sure made everyone else move too. The service was over for the night.

We had one film that we loved to show: it was about Elijah. After one showing of it, word got out rather rapidly. The word was spread that we had said— taking the film somewhat out of context—that it was not going to rain for three years. Those who opposed our coming into the area, and especially the evil one, delighted in enhancing that word and said, "Not going to rain for three years! Liars, liars—we told you so. All they say are lies!" Those types of instances reminded us of the stakes that are involved. The eternal destiny of men and women and boys and girls was involved. There are no stakes higher than those lives. It helped reinforce our commitment to continue sowing the good Word seed.

There is one other trip that we will never forget. We did not always have the luxury of flying into Ilom. Sometimes because of weather or scheduling, we had to postpone a trip. We had decided that because we had made some solid contacts, we had better take advantage of the opportunity to visit Ilom as soon as possible. I asked two of our local Ixil men and the evangelist Pap Lap to come with me on a trip to share God's Word. We had sent word to Ilom a few days before our anticipated arrival and felt that we were returning to Ilom with some confidence. When we rounded one of the bends in the trail about two hours from the village, we saw a young boy coming to meet us. He was about fourteen years old, and when he came up to me, he pulled a live chicken out from under his sweater and gave it to me. My Ixil companions were impressed—this was the ultimate welcome and acceptance gift. It reassured our confidence. The young boy was the grandson of the man to whom I had given the book of Mark.

Imagine the scene later that evening: I was extracting teeth around nine o'clock in the one-room schoolhouse with the usual press of observers around. Men and boys were talking, joking, and kibitzing. They were waiting for me to finish extracting teeth so we could begin the service. Suddenly, a strange silence seemed to fall over the group. I can remember dropping my dental instruments and looking for my Bible. My three other companions all started to give strong witness of who Jesus is and what He is able to do. We bore strong, continual witness for over a half hour. Then, nine Ixil men dropped to their knees and began to confess Jesus as Lord, and they were born again. It was a dramatic manifestation of the Holy Spirit and His power. As St. Paul says, "One sows, another waters but it is God who gives the increase!" (1 Corinthians 3:6, 7). What a blessed experience to be there at the harvest!

"Those that sat in darkness have seen a great light" (Isaiah 9:2). Talk about a drop of a miracle—it was like a cataract. What a difference between this night and the night of the snake slithering among the schoolhouse crowd. I must say, however, that there was some confusion and panic as the Father's mighty hand fell upon us that night. And one man abandoned the grip of grace by leaping out of the window.

Out of that dramatic night came Pap Martin. Pap Martin was the one who had asked me to leave the book of Mark behind, and he now said, "You can use my home, my house when you come, and we can have a part of the house for the 'church' to meet!" He had been touched by the Spirit of God and was now "a new creation." Now, Pap Martin wanted to have a part in making the message of Jesus known in his village.

No more schoolhouse—now it was Pap Martin's front yard, Pap Martin's pine trees, and Pap Martin's house where the drops of miracles would fall. It had become blessed ground!

Isn't it so gracious of our God to give us the wonderful opportunity to be in on some of His spectacular moments? Oh, I know we are always in high expectation of His mighty hand at work, but isn't it great when He lets us in on it? But you and I know that sometimes it comes when we least expect it. And isn't that just like Him?

Oh, yes, about that guy who jumped out of the window—he wound up at Pap Martin's house and experienced that drop of a miracle by accepting Jesus Christ as his Lord and Savior. He was pursued by that marvelous grace; the hound of heaven chased him down.

It is this grace that is not only irresistible, it is dauntless and relentless in its pursuit. You can't escape no matter how hard you try.

CHAPTER 13

Nan Cat

No story about Ilom could be complete without Nan Cat. There she stood, with those enormous black-rimmed glasses, in the crowd of the unofficial greeting committee. She stood out because she was dressed differently. We were in the remote Ixil village of Ilom, but she was dressed in Ladino (or westernized) clothing instead of the traditional Ixil attire, and it was topped off with a large, floral apron. Who was this woman, and why was she here in the village?

It turns out that she had crossed the mountain with her husband seeking a new life and settled in Ilom. Obviously, she was accepted in the community and put down roots. Her husband consumed way too much alcohol. She had three children—two girls and a boy—and for all intents and purposes, she was Mom. Somehow, she eked out an existence, possibly serving a few meals and picking coffee. Her daughters grew, and Nan Cat discovered that they had begun to lose some of their vigor. The years spent living their lifestyle were taking their toll. They were taking their toll upon Nan Cat, too. She was going blind; hence the enormous black-rimmed glasses. The girls were eleven and fourteen when we met them. They seemed to be okay, but we did notice that they were underweight. We also noticed something else: something behind their hollow-looking eyes pleaded for help. Could it be that we were there just for them? The possibility of getting any help for them at that point in time seemed to be impossible. Oh, sure, there was a hospital out there somewhere, but how could we get the girls there? We had swooped in on some harsh reality. We decided that those girls needed some help, and what we had was hope! We offered to fly them out to a hospital. Obviously, Nan Cat was torn with a decision between separation from her children and the hope that they could get better, although no one knew how long that could take, which released a flood of doubt. Her great love for her children overruled. She decided to let them go.

As we flew out of Ilom, we realized as we soared through the valley that we had left a very sad mother behind. It didn't seem long before we were on the ground in the town of Huehuetenago, where we took the two girls to the government hospital. They were diagnosed with tuberculosis. A special hospital in the same town was available to treat the many cases they had at that time. When we turned the two girls over to that hospital, we discovered that it was extremely crowded. We said a very teary goodbye, but we had faith that the girls were going to get better.

What reports we could get out of the hospital were relayed to Nan Cat in Ilom. We knew it must have seemed to be a very long time between news reports on her girls. But do you know what? Those girls got better. Days and weeks and months passed, and they were finally declared well enough to go home.

As we reflect on these events, we are conscious of a mother's great love. We are thankful for the provision of the hospital and the doctors and nurses that cared for Silvia and Rosa. It encourages our faith in how God the Father can arrange an agenda if we trust Him.

As the events unfolded in the lives of Nan Cat's daughters, we cannot help but think about our Father's ability to turn the impossible into the possible. But wait, isn't that what He said? The first disciples were caught up in this amazement and said to each other, "Who then can be saved?" Jesus looked at them and said, "With man this is impossible, but not with God: all things are possible with God" (Mark 10: 26, 27).

CHAPTER 14

Four-Legged Mobility

Every missionary in Guatemala needs a horse. I knew I needed a horse. It's almost like being in Texas and needing a pickup truck. It was a great way to get mobile.

My first horse was small, but he was very mild mannered around the children. I named him Cherokee. Because he was small, he did not have the stamina for the trips that I needed to make. However, I did try to put him to use. Some of our trips to the villages and congregations in the mountains were grueling and put our physical stamina to the test. Returning from one of those trips, Cherokee just ran out of gas. At one point on the trail, he stopped and could hardly stand up he was so exhausted. In fact, it was so bad that I had to actually hold him up for a while as he regained his composure. I felt somewhat in a dilemma because we were still almost a good day's travel from home. After we rested a while, I tried to coax him along, but it was to no avail. Fortunately, we were very close to one of the ranches of one of the men who also had a house in our town. I had seen him on various occasions in town, and he knew of our trips on the trail by his ranch. He had once mentioned to me that if I ever needed anything in my travels, I should not hesitate to stop by. The thought came to me that the only hope I had for Cherokee was to leave him at this ranch so that he could recuperate. I made my way up to the house, which was off the trail, and was fortunate to find the owner at home. I told him my situation with my horse, and he said he would be happy to take care of the horse until he got his strength back. You can believe I felt very relieved. Cherokee must have sensed what we were going to do because I was able to get him to move, albeit very slowly, to the ranch. So I said adios to Cherokee and knew that I was leaving him in good hands. It was over a month before that kind man was able to bring my horse back to town. I knew then it was time for me to look for another horse.

I came to my senses about the next purchase. I realized that I needed someone who knew something about horse flesh, and I knew just the man who would fill the bill. He was a former coffee plantation owner and former mayor who had a great reputation in town. He had such maturity that I felt he knew everything, and his presence on any scene always commanded attention. I approached him and asked his advice and help in purchasing another horse. I was surprised and thrilled with the way don Pedro responded: "I would be delighted to help you. In fact, this is a most opportune time because in the town over the mountains this coming week there is going to be the annual sale and auction coming of horses and mules." So, with don Pedro by my side, I made the trip. I also began to think that maybe I should consider what kind of sure-footed animal I should get for the amount of travel that I planned to do. I discussed this with don Pedro, and he agreed that my best bet was probably a mule.

We arrived at the auction and began to scope out the animals. It did not take us long to discover the mule that he thought would be very good for me. We negotiated the price (I should say, don Pedro negotiated the price), and the deal was sealed. I told don Pedro that my first order of business was to let my new purchase know who is boss. I walked up beside him by the corral where he was tied up and was about to give some commands when all of a sudden, his back feet came off the ground. Those high-flying feet delivered a tremendous punch to my rib cage! It came so swiftly that it caught me completely off guard. I am sure it must have lifted me a few feet off the ground and drove me a few yards back. Fortunately, he did not break any bones, but I sure had a sore rib cage for a while. I am sure also that at the annual auction and roundup, there is still a discussion about the gringo showing who was boss. Now that we knew who the boss was, we began our adventure together. I named him Pompoon.

Pompoon set the pace for our time together. He had all of the aspects and characteristics of a typical mule. He was sure-footed and, boy, how he could play the head game! He put a new meaning into *stubborn*. When I first tied him up with a rope, he ate the rope and then ate about a row of corn in one of my neighbor's fields. I could replace the rope, but I had to pay dearly for the corn. He seemed to be allergic to water. When we approached any size body of water—be it a small stream or a large river—he put on the scared act. When we came to a bridge—forget it. He was not going over it. I thought a few times about building a fire behind him, but that seemed too much effort for what I felt was complete disobedience. I tried to treat him with understanding, compassion, and love, but the more I poured on him the more disgruntled he became. He began to become more temperamental. I just could not get used to thinking of him kicking on every spur of the moment, especially whether he would kick some young child and particularly if that young child was mine. I appreciated don Pedro's insight on horseflesh, but I thought it best to get rid of Pompoon.

Sometimes, the best comes last. I purchased a fine-looking, strong, black horse and named him Sparky. And he did have a lot of spark. He was a great sport. All that Pompoon was, Sparky wasn't. He was great around the kids. Let me share with you one great story about Sparky.

On one occasion, another couple named Bob and Martha (Tita), who were colleagues in the field, came to visit with the purpose of visiting some of the congregations in our area. We planned to use some horses because we intended to do a good bit of traveling in the mountainous areas.

Sparky had been a great traveling companion, and we had built up a good relationship. It was almost like a bonding had taken place in the few years that we had been together. I always took Sparky into town from the pasture the night before a trip. We had a small piece of property in town with a building where the believers from the outlying villages could stay overnight. There was also an empty lot where people could tie up their horses and feed them.

I really trusted my young Ixil friend, Xhel, who worked for us, with making sure Sparky was taken care of the night before a trip. This particular morning, Xhel brought Sparky to the house and tied him to the hitching bar at the window of our home. Our house bordered a couple of main streets, and we had many people walking by our house in the morning. I heard a knock at the door, and my Ixil neighbor informed me that something was wrong with Sparky. He was foaming at the mouth! My neighbor owned horses and sized up the situation.

"It looks like Sparky has had an overdose of corn," he said. "My advice for a quick fix is to run him around the block about five times."

Off we went, running around and around and around the block. When we got back to the house, we were both panting. What a way to wake up!

The next thing I knew, there came another neighbor. He also had some "horse sense" and chimed in with another remedy. He said, "What you have to do is give him a saltwater fix for the real cure. You take a bottle filled with strong saltwater, hold his mouth shut, and pour it down through his nose." Sparky had that wild-eyed look about him as I approached with an elongated snouted whiskey bottle (that I borrowed). I held his mouth shut and—gurgle, gurgle—down it went through his nose. Sparky gave a few snorts and a hearty horse sneeze but no big belches.

Just then another neighbor, a homegrown veterinarian and counselor, showed up. "No, no," he said. "What you really need to do is relieve his stomach. You have to get a big, heavy, thick rope, and then you get on one side of the horse and have someone else on the other side. You put the rope under his belly and begin at his forelegs and work your way back. Very slowly you saw the rope back and forth as you move toward his back legs. Work your way across his belly all the way to his hind legs." I found a big heavy rope, not the tugboat hawser type but I thought big enough to do the job. I got that wild-eyed expression from Sparky again as I tossed the rope under him. We slowly worked our way back under his stomach. We got so into it that we actually lifted Sparky's hind legs off the ground. We heard some grunting from Sparky and thought for sure something would pass—but to no avail. The neighbor shrugged his shoulders and walked off.

We were already behind schedule and thought that perhaps Sparky would walk it off, so we left. After about a kilometer with no cargo, Sparky seemed to be all right. I asked Martha if she would like to mount up, and she said sure. I told her I would walk alongside and keep a close eye on Sparky. A few more kilometers down the road, Sparky still seemed okay. I had no sooner said that to Martha when I noticed that his feet seemed to be sliding. It seemed I was watching a slow-motion film. Right in the middle of a muddy area, Sparky's feet began to slide in a spread-eagle fashion. It was like watching a slowly descending parachute gently collapse. It was such a slow-motion maneuver that Martha was able to gently step off his back, but now I had a horse down in the mud!

A few Ixil men were coming the other way, and they called out, "Get him up! Get him up!" I nudged, coaxed, tugged, pushed, and pulled, and finally Sparky awkwardly stood. "Run him! Run him!" the men shouted again. "Run him down to the watering pool. Make him run, then make him drink!" So, off again we went, running like crazy as I coaxed Sparky on.

We arrived at the watering pool that was a stop for all travelers on the road. When we arrived, trying to catch our breath, other travelers were already there. One Ixil man approached, looked at my horse, and said, "I had a horse like that one time, same symptoms. He died on the trail with me!"

"Let's go, Sparky. Let's get out of here!" I said. I reasoned that if I could keep Sparky moving, I could keep him alive.

Down the trail we went. I was way ahead of the rest of the group. I decided we would rest and wait at a small bridge in the valley. There was a small store at the spot, so I thought that I would visit with the owner while I waited. I told him of the situation with Sparky and his problems of the morning. "Oh," he said, "I had a horse like that once, and guess what I did with him?" I thought, *Wow, it seems like everyone has had a horse like this one at some moment in time, so I can hardly guess.* Before I could answer, he said, "Alka Seltzer." Well, with all I had been through already that morning, I was willing to try anything. I thought, *Whatever it takes.* I got four Alka Seltzers down Sparky without any effort.

When the rest of the group arrived, they did not believe what I had done. We waited for a little while before we made the climb up to the chapel building where we would hold that night's service.

I tied Sparky outside of the chapel building, and as a service began, I spoke about the problem with my horse. Almost everyone seemed to relate to it, so I said, "I don't know how you feel about praying for animals, but I'm going to pray for my horse right now." And I asked God to heal Sparky.

We went on with the usual service and fellowship. After it was over, I went out to check on Sparky, and he seemed to be okay, as did the rest of the horses we had with us. The next morning, we set off to another new village higher up the mountain range. Sparky seemed to be as good as ever. In fact, when I walked behind him as he climbed the mountain that morning with Martha on his back, he seemed stronger than ever.

Sparky continued to serve in a special way. He was part of the drops of a miracle that we experienced in our travels. He was also part of the sparks of the good news that were fanned into flames that changed men and women and boys and girls forever. When we had to leave Guatemala, I gave Sparky to the Ixil evangelist, Jose. I knew that he would be in good hands and would continue to serve. I also gave Jose the saddle, the bridle, the halter, ropes, the cargo seat, and a box of Alka Seltzer.

CHAPTER 15

The Mountain Goat

The Mountain Goat was passed on to me by my predecessor, Rev. Fred Parkyn. Fred, in his day, wanted to get mobile too. He made a lot of inquiries to a lot of companies and learned about a glorified moped out there. It was actually a five-horsepower Briggs & Stratton motor bolted to a thick steel plate on a frame of strongly welded pipes. It had a terrific gear ratio; it had only one. A heavy-duty drive chain ran from the motor sprocket to the back-wheel sprocket. The tire on the back was large and wide, and a small, narrow tire sat on the front. Only a front-wheel brake was installed, and no lights were available. It was some sturdy animal and could climb a tree—I was to discover that later. It also had a durable rack on the back. I've heard that hunters used it in the state of Washington to haul deer out of the mountains. Fred went to great effort to get it purchased, shipped to Guatemala, and out of the customs house. He was an innovator, a mover and a shaker. He moved from our area to a new ministry at the Utatlan School and decided that he did not need the Mountain Goat to ride herd on the students at the new school. So, I was the benefactor of his means of spreading the good news.

I am sure that Fred had many stories about the Mountain Goat. I had my share, too.

When I first began to negotiate a few trial runs with the

Mountain Goat, I found it decent to handle. So I set out on my first visit to a village. I packed a few items on the back rack, and because it was a nice day, I tied my sweater around my waist. Up the trail I went for a three-hour ride. I discovered, however, after the first hour that I felt something kind of tugging at my back. When I stopped to take a break, I realized that the dangling sweater had been caught in the back sprocket and chain, and they had begun to chew and unknit my sweater. About half of it had disappeared, and I looked rather weird with only two dangling sweater arms wrapped around my waist. I learned not to do that again.

I wanted to have Elaine with me on the next adventure with the Mountain Goat on a trip to a village. I did not want her to miss out on the thrill of the ride. Now, with our trails and roads under a barrage of rain, the adventure became more tantalizing with excitement. I loaded the back rack with lunch, a gas can, and some extra clothes and rain gear. We had a word of prayer and began our journey out of town. The first thing that popped off the rack was the gas can. The next thing that came off was our lunch. The final blow was when I was trying to negotiate through a puddle (pond!) and, with just a little awkward movement, down we went. Fortunately, Elaine had bailed and missed a lot of the mud. As I retrieved the Goat and the extra clothes out of the mud, I drove the Mountain Goat up out of the murky waters. I told Elaine that I would go on up above the bad spot and wait. When I got a few yards up the trail, I looked back and discovered she was heading in the other direction back to town. It seems that she had had enough of our venture together on the Mountain Goat. She called out to me, "Have a great trip. See you when you get back. Love you! God bless!"

I had another adventure with the Mountain Goat one day when I took a young man with me to visit another village. We left early in the morning and arrived at the village without any incident. We were sharing with the people in the village and then realized that time had gotten away from us. We needed to hurry back to our town before it got dark. (As I mentioned earlier, the Mountain Goat had no lights!) A rain shower had passed through earlier, and I was a little concerned. As we got to the top of one of the slippery, clay-based trails, darkness overtook us. I felt confident, however, that we could make it down the long, steep hill without any problems. Once we got started, however, I noticed that it was a lot more slippery than I had anticipated. I had forgotten about the chickens and their agility. (remember the saying for our town: 'Why sometimes even a chicken can't stand up!') My companion on the back was holding on to me and the flashlight. I applied the brake, but it seemed like the tire had turned into a ski and was actually giving us more momentum. We were picking up more speed. There were a lot of trees on both sides of the trail. I panicked. I knew that it was time for my companion to abandon ship. I also knew he really only understood Ixil. Panic did what panic does, and I called out in English, "Jump! Jump off!" Before the last syllable was out, Xhel was gone! I have never had a ride so thrilling in my life. Down, down the trail I sped in the darkness, with my stomach in my throat. A thought flashed through my mind—*Well, at least someone will be alive to tell what happened!* Somehow, I slalomed through that course, missed all the trees, and finally came to a stop at the river bridge. I breathed a sigh of relief. (Talk about an understatement!) It was definitely a drop of a miracle. Xhel would not get back on; he ran alongside the slow moving Mountain Goat with a flashlight in hand for the next hour before we reached home. I am sure that for him, it must have been the ride of his life before he bailed. I wonder sometimes if, when Xhel is sitting around the fire with his friends and family, what he tells them about the night when the "Mus" (non-Ixil) disappeared into the darkness.

I remember another experience that also occurred at night. We got word one day that a leader in the church in Chajul had died. In our culture, quick burial is called for, which means that a wake is held on the day of death and the next day the burial occurs. So we knew that we had to try to get there that day if we were to make our presence known and to share our concern and love. If I traveled at night, I liked to have a companion, and this particular day I got a great one.

Rodolfo was one of those full-grown gangly men—you know, the Abe Lincoln type. His long legs would help stabilize the Mountain Goat as we negotiated through the ruts and potholes of the dirt roads. On this particular day, we were also faced with a lot of rain. So, in the name of the Lord, we began our journey. I don't know how many times we slipped and slid in the trucks' and buses' ruts. I do know that Rodolfo had great agility and stamina. He had those long legs moving from one side to the other saving us from spills. There were a few times, however, when he was not up to the challenge, but we arrived without any major injuries. We were soaked and full of mud, and the only thing that we really needed was a change of clothes, which of course we didn't have. When Rodolfo got up to speak, he said in a tone of voice that seemed to hold an anxiety release, "Praise God, we arrived safely." To me, it gave a whole new meaning to that phrase. Then, standing there in his rain-soaked clothes and mud-caked shoes, Rodolfo poured his heart out in a challenging, comforting, powerful word from the Word. A special touch of the Spirit was evident, and it was powerful for the grieving family. Isn't that how He works when you couple Him with the Word? It was worth the trip!

I wish I had some stories of great heroic effort with the Mountain Goat—you know, where I go in, rescue people in a village, drag them out on a travois with the Mountain Goat to safety, and save their lives. But how do you measure success? The Mountain Goat was given and used in the name of the Lord Jesus and for His kingdom. Maybe someday, we will hear someone say,

> I saw a strange-looking moped coming my way.
>
> And I didn't run away.
>
> And those on that Mountain Goat pointed me to the Way.
>
> Praise God, I arrived safely!

After all, in a sense, isn't everything sacred?

Sure, the Mountain Goat got me around, but I got the feeling that I got closer to the people by walking. So I relinquished the Goat to another part of the field. That Mountain Goat had the distinct and unique privilege of arriving to the top of the volcano Santa Maria in Quetzaltenango, albeit taken apart and carried the last one-half mile up to the top. The Anderson boys put it back together and posed for a historical picture before coming back down.

Now about that climbing tree experience. That's a story for another time.

CHAPTER 16

I Began to Think

I began to think, *Things are changing in Ixil country. New roads are opening up into new areas.* Our Chevy Suburban had been performing well for many of the tasks at hand, but many tasks were reserved for a four-wheel drive. Several of our trips in the Suburban were made after I opened the tailgate and tossed in a shovel, an *azadon*, an ax, chains, a jack, and boards. The boards were pressed into service after the car was jacked up to make a bridge or road. I began to think a four-wheel-drive vehicle would be ideal. A Jeep, maybe, would be good to get into some of the areas and, of course, continue to reach the areas we were already ministering in.

So I began to think again: *We are going to the States for the denomination's conference sessions (and incidentally, to get ordained!). We could present a project to the mission board for a four-wheel-drive vehicle.* As we shared our vision with others, we were warned to be prepared for attitudes like, "We have never done that before" and "That does not seem to be in the budget." We prayed and put a presentation together to share with the board. I thought it would be a good idea to share a huge map of Ixil country and the opportunities that would be made available with a four-wheel-drive vehicle.

The day came for my audience and presentation. I got to the room ahead of time and put up the map of Ixil country. The board members came and started their sessions to discuss and make decisions concerning mission business. Finally, I was called in to give my report. I shared with the board the tremendous blessings that the Lord Jesus had laid on us in Ixil country. Men and women and families were coming to Christ, and churches and leaders were being raised up. Then, I gave them a glimpse of the opportunities we had and described how much a four-wheel-drive vehicle would facilitate further ministry. I went to the map and showed some of the new roads and villages that could be reached. And, yes, the comments that we had been warned about came out: "Great idea, but the mission board has never done this before," "We have never bought a vehicle for a missionary or a ministry," and "We don't want to set a precedent." I could see and feel that the attitude was drifting toward refusal.

But then, one pastor, Reverend Collins, on the mission board was legally blind. In fact, I almost tripped over his seeing-eye dog as I enthusiastically scoped the map on the wall for them. Reverend Collins began to speak, "I can see this vision of Missionary Lawrence. Why don't we see if we can raise some money right here at the conference to facilitate this ministry?" The board agreed! A blind man had seen the vision!

The next day, someone from a nearby farm loaned his Jeep for fund-raising. We parked it in front of the church, and with the Elaine standing alongside it and clothed in full Ixil regalia, which we happened to have with us, the fundraiser began. By the end of conference sessions, we had enough money to buy the vehicle *and* keep it maintained for a while. It was not because we thought that we so desperately needed it but that the Father willed it to be.

When we returned to Guatemala, we bought the vehicle. The Lord does not do anything halfway. This was first class—we had enough money to buy a Land Rover. What a vehicle! And later we got a winch for the front bumper and chains for all four wheels. It could go anywhere, even where sure-footed mules feared to tread. It was unstoppable.

The rest is history. And *what* a history—moving the sick, bringing the medical clinic to the villages, and taking equipment like the movie projector to the villages, and sowing the good news of Jesus has all been made possible with this car. It was great for the believing community to know that they had that type of vehicle available to and for them.

Once, when a new road was inaugurated, we were invited to follow the governor into the village and cut the ribbon and then share in a special fiesta feast to celebrate the new road. We had the opportunity that afternoon to present the claims of Jesus Christ and declare Him as the Way. In another village, we were invited to show films on the life of Christ. As we were operating the projector on top of the Land Rover, showing the film against the whitewashed side of the schoolhouse, a sudden Guatemalan thunderstorm came up. We quickly tried to protect the projector by spreading a canvas over the top, and we continued to show the film. We had been so anxious to cover the machine that we did not notice that the people were still standing in the pouring rain.

I remember one instance when there was a frantic knock at the door. The man quickly informed me that there was an emergency. A family of five—father and mother and three children—had inadvertently eaten some bad mushrooms. It was a panicky appeal for us to do something. When we arrived at the house, the consensus was that these people needed to get to the hospital as quickly as possible. I dashed home and started the Land Rover, I returned to the house, and we quickly loaded the family in the Land Rover. Off we sped with a prayer and the hope of arriving at the hospital in time. You would have to appreciate the trip that we were making—we traveled over thirty minutes on the mountain road, another forty-five minutes across the ridge, and then another forty-five minutes down to the river valley of Sacapulas. We would then cross the bridge and still face other two hours of driving to get to the hospital. One of the luxuries that we forfeited with the super stable Land Rover was a comfortable ride over the mountainous roads. Little did I realize that we were going to be experiencing a progressive healing. As the Land Rover jostled over the roads, the family began to feel woozy, and some of them began to throw up. As we were on our way across the ridge, others threw up too. And as we descended the switchbacks down to the river valley, I would dare to say that everyone had thrown up. And do you know what? When we stopped to rest at the bridge, everyone felt a lot better—including the driver. In fact, they said they were okay and that there was no need to go on to the hospital. What can I say? It was a drop of a miracle. I turned the Land Rover around and headed back toward home.

I think that you can appreciate that there were many, many more kilometers put on the Land Rover in the name of the Lord Jesus and to His glory. It was involved in the cement block-making efforts. It pulled the block plant off the eighteen-wheeler and onto the concrete platform. It spent some months hauling sand for that block plant. The Land Rover sure did add another dimension to the ministry.

Obviously, the Land Rover brought a lot of new opportunities to our ministry. We were able to take advantage of invitations and to be in more places more often. Obviously, this ability also brought more pressure on our time schedule. Those invitations, that knock on the door late at night, the needs—how many more jobs will be added? But we were ready and willing to perform the tasks that were needed to keep the ministry and a Land Rover functioning in the role that it should play in our diversified program. It certainly extended and accelerated our ministry. We realized, however, that that need cried out. We began to face the reality that we were not going to be able to keep up with all of the needs. I think in one way the Land Rover somewhat set the stage for us to begin to think about and pursue ways to meet some of those needs.

CHAPTER 17

I Began to Think Again: An Ambulance Comes to Town

When the Land Rover arrived, it thrust into our faces the reality that we were not going to be able to keep up with all the demands of the ministry. It was pretty obvious that I was not going to be able to maintain all of my new responsibilities. There was just not enough time or personnel to cover all the bases. How could we facilitate multiplying ourselves and delegate some tasks? There was an overwhelming need in the area of first responders for medical issues and then transporting patients to the hospital.

We kept praying, and one of the ideas we came up with was to tap the resources closest to us—the church and the townspeople. Okay, great idea, but how were we going to go about doing that?

Was there an organization out there that we could ask for help? We discovered that some towns had volunteer fire departments. They were not so much full-blown fire departments with fire trucks, but at least they had ambulances (pick-up with a camper top) and first-aid responders. We decided to look into that. We went to the capital to discuss our situation with the national Guatemalan fire department. This was a paid, professional organization connected to the government, and they were delighted to be able to help us. They had experience in helping many of the other towns and villages, and we saw some great advantages in being connected with them. We would be under their umbrella and have all the credentials, the government backing, and the connections. Along with that came training, subsidized gas, and other help we might need. They would be willing to send their professionals to our town to train all of our volunteers. Now, all that we needed was a place to call the fire station and a vehicle. There was no problem at all with getting a piece of property in town. The town officials were highly in favor of our endeavor because they knew the needs of their people. That ride out of town to the hospital over the dirt roads might finally be solved.

Well, we had made the first move, and at least we had an organization that was credible and that would back us up. We had our local location, and now all we needed was the vehicle. We needed to get some wheels under our vision.

We had another opportunity to go to the States, and we had packed the vision in our hearts. We thought that this would be a great opportunity to present our vision of the ambulance to our hometown. There is nothing like a hometown church atmosphere. When we were in Maryland, we attended the church that Elaine had gone to when she was younger. It was in this church that we began to share the vision. (Incidentally, Elaine's hometown church, Waugh Methodist, was the featured church in the movie *Runaway Bride*.) The pastor of the church, Rev. Paul Grant, jumped on the vision. We also shared that same vision with our Primitive Methodist conference and our friends. Our good friends in New Bedford, Massachusetts, Gil and Arlene, were the first ones to send us a check. That check coming in the mail was a great encouragement to us. The next thing we knew, the two churches in Maryland, Waugh and Fork (they were on a circuit), really took on the project. Time ran its course for us in the States, and we returned to Guatemala. We wondered when we settled in our home in Nebaj how the ambulance project would turn out.

A few months later, we got a letter from Reverend Grant. It went like this:

> Greetings in the name of the Lord. I hope this letter finds you and your family in good health. The Lord has been doing miraculous things in our midst. I know this ambulance truck has been His will for your people and ours. Funds for this project have come in beyond belief at the writing of this letter. We have raised over $2,225 for the project. A total stranger called Monday and said he had the vehicle we were looking for. The cost is $2,300. We will have that money in a few days. We have looked at it and are satisfied that it will do the job. It is a '71 Ford pickup with a cap on the back and heavy-duty suspension. We have told them that we want it. Both churches held a rock-a-thon. It was a 24-hour rocking chair event where the kids got sponsors for a donation for an hour of rocking. This project was so interesting in our area that a TV station out of Baltimore stopped by to give it a news interview. They broadcast some of the event live. In my life, I never remember any church programming receiving this kind of coverage. People stopped in and just gave money. We have realized over $700 today and expect $400 more to come in tomorrow.
>
> We are now trying to ascertain the procedure for getting the truck to you. We want to get it there the best way—in any event, I know it will all work out not because it is my will or yours, but God desires it to be so. With his warmest blessings, I remain, sincerely, Paul.

With the news from the church we decided to put in motion the how-to part of getting the vehicle to us. Obviously, we needed a few drivers to drive it down. Morgan Hoover, my former scoutmaster and friend; Reverend Grant; and a young man who just decided he wanted to ride along became the team of drivers. Remember that the means of communication in our town was a telegraph and telegrams. Phone calls were rare and only to close locations. Now, we had to put together some type of an agenda. We needed to anticipate the arrival time at the border with Mexico. We gave them the route to drive down through the States, through Texas, and then down through Mexico to the border with Guatemala. I sent them a list of what to do to prepare for the crossing into Mexico and where to get insurance. I tried to give them a little advice about the border crossing. Obviously, we could not see or plan for any unforeseen difficulties. We had arranged that in a certain town in Mexico, a day before they were to reach the Guatemalan border, they would send me a telegram of their location and estimated time that they would arrive. Believe me—we were in great anticipation of their coming.

The telegram arrived, and we went to meet them at the border. Morgan was a railroad engineer, and they were running right on schedule. For the border crossing into Guatemala, we had all the documents and the legal papers certified and stamped by the Guatemalan fire department and the Guatemalan government. The document was red ribbon decorated, wax sealed, and stamped with gold stamps. The officials had put all the authority in the document that they could muster with all the dramatic flowing, flowery signatures. That document whisked us through immigration and customs like some magical hand. We zipped through; it was the most impressive border crossing I ever experienced. It was a preview of what was about to happen and what we were to experience in our hometown of Nebaj. We had no idea what kind of reception was in store for us.

It was dusk when we arrived at our town. When we drove the vehicle down the street through the entrance of our town, literally thousands of people had turned out, and we could hardly get through the streets. That never-to-be-forgotten night was enhanced by flower petals that were strewn over the vehicle and in front of it as we drove down the street to the local Primitive Methodist church. There were so many fireworks that they blew the limbs and branches off the pine trees on the streets in the park. The words of welcome and deep appreciation from the mayor, the town officials, the pastors, and the local church leaders overwhelmed us. It was a good thing that we had a little time to recover because, the following night, we had a special dedication service in the town hall. One of the Ixil Mayan leaders stood and spoke, saying, "This day we have seen the visible demonstration of God's great love, power, and grace." As that man spoke, I thought back to that letter from Reverend Grant, where he said, "The ambulance is coming to Nebaj, not because you want it to be or because I wanted it to be, but that God wants it to be so."

Reverend Grant concluded his speech to the community in the town hall that night by saying, "I hope that each one of you when you see the ambulance go by will be reminded that God loves you through Jesus Christ." And isn't that what it is all about. Haven't you heard?

Our town of Nebaj was never the same again because we saw so dramatically God's creative power and love at work. The believers' stock rose ten thousand points. I had people talking to me who early on wouldn't even say hi. Now I had a closer personal opportunity to share just what our God can do. What an increase of our faith!

The new volunteer group came together and began to jell. The young men and the older guys in our town were enthusiastic about joining the cause. The professionals from the capital came and did the training. I felt that I had to be involved, so I took the training along with them. It was a great opportunity for me also to make more contacts. Then, finally, came the day when we graduated and were handed our credentials, along with handshakes and ranks. I was surprised that I received an honorary captain's membership. I had said at the beginning that I would be committed up to a point in time but then I would have to get back to my other responsibilities.

They seemed to understand, and I really greatly appreciated all that the professionals from the capital did for us. I was impressed with our young people and the town leaders who stepped up with great commitment. What they did for us and what they were doing for our community was a great blessing.

A few months later, I wrote a prayer and thank you letter to those who were supporting us. The letter said,

> We had a great Christmas and New Year's Day. I had the duty in regard to the ambulance on Christmas Day. I had two trips and I did not get home until 11:00 PM but we did get to eat Christmas dinner together between trips. For us, it was a real sense of satisfaction and fulfillment to see the ambulance in action. It continues today as a real blessing. We averaged about one service call a day. Many of these calls I would be doing, so you can see it has relieved me to do other things. I began to think, you know, it couldn't be working better even if I would've planned it that way!

The day came when I was relieved of my position with the volunteer firemen. I did, however, consent to be the treasurer for another two years. It was sort of nice when I walked through the streets of the town and was greeted with a salute and "Good morning, my captain!"

I know in the depths of my heart, however, who the real Captain is, and He deserves all the credit!

CHAPTER 18

Airstrip

We were really getting mobile, what with horses, the Land Rover, the Mountain Goat, the ambulance, and even an airplane.

But I began to think, it sometimes took us four to five hours to get to the landing strip to begin that thirty- or forty-five-minute plane ride to our destinations. There were airstrips close to our colleagues and that seemed to be good for them, but my thought was that we needed an airstrip in our town.

Dream on, dreamer! I told myself. *In your town nestled in the rugged mountainous terrain? Fat chance! And just think of the weather that you face.* But then I reasoned that, while the area is certainly rugged at ground level, what about from a bird's-eye view? Could there be a flat spot that is straight and long enough? I began to talk to Bill Overhulser about the idea, and he thought it was great and said he would fly up and scope the area. Sure enough, when Bill flew over our area, he noticed a perfect spot.

Now, our next step was to share the idea with the mayor and the town officials. They also thought it was a grand idea and jumped on a plan. The idea quickly spread; it went to the department capital and then on to the Guatemalan government in the capital city. Our credibility stood up, and they approved the plan. Our local town hall and mayor began to negotiate for the land. Getting all the Mayan

Indian landowners to agree to sell was a task in itself, especially when you take into consideration their concept of the land. Some were unhappy. But the price was right, and progress ruled the day. We received continual approval and cooperation from the government, and they decided that the road crew in that area would actually do the earth moving, the grading, and the finishing touches to the airstrip. The government came and did all the survey work. To demonstrate our great satisfaction with how things were progressing, our mission gave a donation; even Bill Overhulser kicked in.

We waited for the dozer and trucks to come—and we waited, and we waited. The survey crew finished its work and left. One day, some trucks from the road crew came. Another crew came and some trees were cut down, but still we saw no dozer.

Then, one night as we were returning from the capital and I made that last turn at the fork in the road that led to our town, I began to notice something different about the road. The headlights began to bring into focus something very different, what seemed to be huge, cleat-like imprints on both sides of the road. It looked like tracks a tank would make. Then it dawned on me: A Caterpillar D8 bulldozer had just passed by. Our airstrip was to become a reality!

The airstrip began to fulfill its mission. As soon as it was finished—well, almost finished anyway—Bill was the first to land on the strip. We were not ready for his arrival. I can remember being in the Navy Seabees and building an airstrip in the Philippines. When we were almost finished, we had to park earthmovers on the runway to keep the army guys from beating the navy to the first landing. I guess pilots have that thing—they are a different breed. But Bill had enough credentials and credibility to eliminate any hassles from the government. He landed his helio and took off again. Then, the finishing touches were added to the strip. Our first ministry visits were from dentists from Texas when they flew in and served our community.

We were blessed with another pilot, Don Donaldson. He flew us and our colleagues all over the field. Don began to fly into our town bringing doctors and nurses from our Chichicastenango hospital. They came with a full package of a mobile clinic.

Early in the day on one of their visits, the weather began to deteriorate rapidly. Everyone got a little antsy as ominous clouds came over the mountains. They made haste to pack up, and Don prepared to fly them out. As I was driving back home, I got stopped on the road by some Ixil people who told me that my neighbor had an emergency. When I arrived at our house, people were huddled around my neighbor's house and mine. It seems he had become an innocent victim of the conflict in our area. At that time, there was an unusual instability in our area. The embers that fuel civil war were being fanned into a blaze. The political power struggles, the inequities in the standard of living, and just the general unrest in some of the status quo fed the fire. Anyway, violence had erupted. The government's army began to make a more visible presence in our area, and the revolutionary forces began to fight back. One of the ways that the revolutionary army did this was by planting Claymore mines on some of the trails and roads. My neighbor, on his way to his cornfield, tripped one, and *boom!* It almost blew his leg off. Fortunately, some people were close by, and they put him on some boards and carried him into town. That's the way I found him in front of his house. He was still on the boards and bleeding. I surveyed the situation and knew he needed help that we were unable to give. What to do? I could still hear the drone of Don's plane as it crossed over the mountain. I had a radio in the house, so I called Don about our emergency. He replied that he would drop the doctors and nurses off at the airstrip in Quiche and return as soon as possible. He did mention, however, that the weather did not look good. I confirmed that on my end, too, the clouds and the rain were beginning to block us in. "I'll head for the airstrip," I said, "as soon I can get Luis loaded in the Land Rover."

More people came in an array of well-wishers. We appreciated all the concern, but they were somewhat impeding my departure for the airstrip. I said, "We must go!" all the while looking skyward with a lot of pessimism. No sooner had that thought run through my head than, out of that low cloud cover and rain, Don flew right over the house and rattled the tiles. Believe me, we made a very rapid trip to the airstrip. Luis was loaded into the plane with his wife, and off they went.

Don told me later that he radioed ahead to the capital's hospital, and they had an ambulance ready to meet him at the Guatemalan City airport. That airlift of Luis off to the hospital in the capital saved his life. In about a month, he came home, and the family was extremely grateful for our help. From that time on, they were open to spiritual conversation and very sensitive to what we had to say. Luis asked me later for spiritual counsel. Because of the spiritual realm in which he lived, he felt that someone had put a hex on him. It seemed that some neighbor had wanted his land and had gone to his religious practitioner to seek otherworldly help in carrying out his plan to acquire it. Only those who have lived in that type of spiritual atmosphere can appreciate the oppression that Luis was under. I was able to share with Luis that Jesus's people live in a different realm. I told him we live in a kingdom where King Jesus is in charge. Jesus had the answer for that hex. By His power, He could just block it out. That was good news for Luis. He told me he felt relieved and was going to think more about Jesus. I relinquished Luis to the Holy Spirit, knowing that He does a much better about bringing conviction than I could ever do.

As I thought about the airstrip, its history, and all of the effort that went into making it happen, I was confirmed in my heart that it was worth the effort. I also thought about those pilots, especially Don and Bill. My heart goes out to them with a hearty "God bless them!" Risking their lives and putting it all on the line for Jesus and His kingdom certainly challenges me! The above story could be told over and over again in the lives of those missionary pilots.

Drops of a miracle come off their wings.

CHAPTER 19

Economy Economics Economize

No matter how you slice it or dice it, the bottom line is currency, money, *dinero, puaj*. Obviously, there is a lot of talk today about the economy. How did that affect a missionary in the highlands of Guatemala? Let me answer that with an excerpt from a letter from a missionary in Indonesia that appeared in the *Alliance Witness* many years ago.

> While the gifts were tangible and have been most generous, I must emphasize prayer. Money cannot create spiritual hunger; it cannot bring about the conviction of sin. It does not call men and women into leadership nor does money have the ability to produce a witnessing Church. It does not give strength to carry an overload of work.

I presume that missionaries scattered over the entire world would voice an "Amen." And those missionaries could add illustration after illustration of God's dramatic work as he touched people and met spiritual, physical, and material needs. Yes, that is just the way He is. Let me share with you a few of my experiences of how God touched lives.

We were down to our last month at home in the States when we realized that, with the many things that we had accumulated, not only for ourselves but for some of the various ministries on our field—the school, the hospital, the camp—we were going to need a trailer to pack and pull all the things to Guatemala. Now, we know that Christians are not supposed to be anxious, but as our departure date loomed closer and there was no trailer in sight, we became a little anxious. Then, one Sunday afternoon, God's people responded. It was during a casual conversation; in fact, the conversation was so casual that I cannot remember exactly what was said. But this man said something like this: "If I can't find a trailer for you, I'll build one!" The interesting upshot of this was that he in fact couldn't find one, so he built one! He was a manual arts teacher at a high school, and he convinced the school to take on the project of building us a trailer. Can you imagine—a public high school manual arts class building a trailer for an evangelical missionary? I am not sure that this would fly in our society today. In those days it seemed things were a little different. We left Maryland pulling a brand-new homemade trailer with a dedicatory plaque attached to its side that read "Presented by A. I. Rigger and Son." What a blessing! Well, we sure did not have the money to pay for that trailer, but God in His economy made it happen.

The ambulance that came to Nebaj had a completely different story. We discovered after a few trips that the set of rims and tires on the ambulance were not available in Guatemala. We treated those tires with TLC, but we knew someday we would have to replace them. A few months later, we made a trip to the States and decided to invest in some new rims and tires. Some friends of ours from an Episcopal church wanted to invest in our ministry by paying for the rims and tires. We were delighted that they were so willing to engage, and I decided that I really couldn't ask them for more in terms of shipping the rims and tires to Guatemala. I just had that feeling that God the Father would supply. So we drove from Maryland to the Jersey Shore, where the shipping warehouse was. I filled out all of the documents, and the bill came to $460. It was almost as much as the cost of the rims and tires themselves. I got a quizzical look on my face that said, *now who is going to pay for this?* Well, by faith I wrote out the check and under my breath breathed out the words, "Jehovah-Jireh." Actually, months went by before a man in Wisconsin was touched. The mission board treasurer included $460 in our support one month and said it had come from someone in Wisconsin who knew we had a need—a drop of a miracle in God's economy.

Then there was the case of my son, Paul, who had been diagnosed with dyslexia. Elaine had a cousin who happened to be involved in special education in the States, and she suggested that we come to the States for more thorough testing. So off Paul and Elaine went. Believe me—this was a step of faith! Looking at our financial sheet, we were not in the position to part with the money for the flight and the testing. "Oh, you of little faith!" Once again, we experience that special touch from the Father as He touched someone else and that person responded to our need by giving a healthy offering to pay the expenses. This special gift also came a few months later after we had stepped out in faith. Can you imagine how we felt when we saw this special amount that was added to our monthly support?

We had a special fund called the Good Samaritan fund that we could draw on whenever there was a special need. We tried to keep a good balance in the fund, but you can imagine that being surrounded by so many needs, the fund always needed replenishing. Many times, we used it for some of the patients who we took to the hospital in Chichicastenango. After I had left one of the patients there, I got word that he was well enough to come home. I sent a telegram that I would be there the next day to pick him up. I knew the hospital needed the space and also would need the money for his stay. I don't know what I was expecting, but I drove off from Nebaj with zero dollars in the Good Samaritan fund. When I arrived at the hospital, I kind of hemmed and hawed about payment. We had a very understanding nurse who graciously said, "I understand. We can wait a few days." I said, "I will get you the money as soon as I can" and drove off with the patient. When I arrived home in Nebaj, I was greeted by Elaine as she was talking to a few French tourists. She said to me that the tourists had asked to look around town at some of the ministries that we have. I said, "You know what, I just have too many things to do right now. I have some very pressing good works I have to do, and I have to also go to this church service at the edge of the village." In my thinking, of course, my agenda was much more important than showing some curious tourists around, so I convinced Elaine to take on the task. We went our separate ways. Later on, that evening, I asked Elaine how everything went. She told me that she had a good time showing the French tourists around and that they seemed to be genuinely interested in the ministry and especially in the clinics. That interest took on a very tangible aspect. They had handed Elaine a hefty offering for the medical ministry. As we counted out the money, I realized it was the amount I needed to pay the hospital for the patient I had brought home. Distance, time, nationality, shortsighted missionary—the Father covers them all. When would I learn?

After the ambulance came to town, there was, of course, a need for money to maintain it. We were connected with the fire department of Guatemala, so we had a very good base for organization and support. They came to town and helped us organize an official fire company with officers and even dedicated them in the town hall. Beyond that, they offered a monthly token of monetary support. They expected us, however, to become self-supporting, so we began to try to raise some money in our town. Well, there was just not a lot of money to go around. One of our fundraisers involved four men holding the corners of a sheet and running through the plaza, the marketplace, and the streets on market day. The object was to have people toss in coins as they trotted by. It also helped keep our volunteer firemen in shape. I happened to be the elected treasurer in those early years, and I can remember sitting at the kitchen table with my wife as we counted all of the nickels, dimes, and many pennies. I think those of you who have served as treasurer of any organization can appreciate the anxieties of the shortfall. And sometimes, what was needed to make up for the shortfall came out of our pockets. But it made me aware that the town was doing its best to support a worthy cause, and for that reason I was encouraged to do the best that I could do with the Father's help. I knew that anything done in His name for His glory would be honored by Him, and I knew that the drops would come, even if it was a penny at a time.

I could mention more of the Father's unique provisions. "Oh, what a coincidence" became a pattern of His special love and concern. But I begin to think of even bigger issues.

There isn't enough money to make Casico burn up his idols. There isn't enough money to pay for Luis to slosh through the mud and rain and the threats to reach his people. There isn't enough money to condition a man's soul to make and respond to the Word and say it's the sweetest thing that ever fell on his heart.

Of course, money is important. Money can do a lot! It paid our support on the mission field and the support of evangelists who were spreading the Word. Money built our hospital in Chichicastenango. Money built and continues to build our Utatlan schools in Quiche. Money kept our clinics open, kept our Bible school open, and kept our Land Rover running. Money is needed and necessary. However, as I have heard it said, "Only God's power can do God's work, and that is released by prayer."

"Pray on every occasion," said Paul. "In the power of the Spirit do this and keep watch and persevere, always interceding for all of God's people; and pray for me that I might be granted the right words when I open my mouth, and may boldly and feely make known His hidden purposes" (Ephesians 6:18–19). Keep praying, praying partners; that's where the power is released.

Perhaps some wonder how those people knew to respond by

giving and to give in a certain amount. After talking to some people concerning this issue, I have come to a conclusion: these people are so in tune to the Holy Spirit of God, and through prayer and their relationship with Him, they are open to what He says. After all, you know, He only does and says what the Father wants and to bring glory to the Son Jesus. What God the Spirit says to them they take at face value, they believe what He says, and what they hear they act on. I don't fully understand how all this works—but I do know that it works!

I don't know how it is with you, but sometimes I am nudged by the Spirit to do certain things and some of those things are in the area of giving. Sometimes I hear about the results, and sometimes I don't. But I feel that the issue is not whether I hear about anything but that I obey. I have to admit, however, that sometimes I don't obey and I'm the one who misses the blessing.

I just want to leave some ideas about God's economy. I know it is extravagant. I know I should always leave a budget with a margin of faith. I know, as someone has said, "God's work done in God's time will never lack God's provision." I know all that; now I need to put it into practice!

CHAPTER 20

Reflect

Have you ever gotten to a point in your life when you were able to take some moments and reflect on some very meaningful experiences or situations? Were you able to return to that place in your mind's eye and conjure up vivid images of how you reacted to those situations? Were you able to gain some insight into how you profited from the experience? Sometimes what you did in a situation somewhat grows on you in a cruel way and creates feelings of pessimism and defeat. If you get into that situation again, it is as if you have blinders on and you cannot seem to react in the way that you feel that you really should. Then you have the opportunity to separate yourself from where you live, move, and interact and the situations you were involved in. You get a chance to reflect on the ifs, the ands, and the buts and even the would have been, could have been, and should have been. You have the liberty to be freed up and to reflect without pressure.

In our instance, we went to the States for a few months, leaving behind the demands and needs in our home and town and countryside. We had some time to reflect with the Father about our call and our continued efforts in Ixil country. Sometimes you just have to pull away. Then you discover that there is nothing like being in His presence to set some issues straight. The shadows and waves of doubt dissipate. You get a new perspective of your call and the stakes involved. I was reminded again as He spoke to me, "Just keep sowing and leave the results to Me!" (see Luke 8:4–15).

With renewed affirmation, we returned to the highlands of Guatemala, our town, and our home and began my reality check. Things seemed to be different than they were before—but were they really? Were the lights really that dim? Were the roads really that bad? Did it really rain that hard in our town? Did I really breathe that hard going up the mountain? And I really wasn't carrying that much either. (Twenty extra pounds of US food didn't help much.)

I can't remember missing my children so much. I cannot remember all of the lights going out at once in the capital city. Even in the hospital, the auxiliary lighting went off, and of all times, during Elaine's operation.

Were the people really that sick? Were the people really that poor? Did the coffee with the hot chili always taste that hot? Did all the Ixil children look that cute? Were the plural Ixil command forms all always that hard? Were the people so hungry for the Word? Were there always so many places and people to visit?

Did I ever feel so useless before without His powerful Spirit working in my heart and life and in the hearts and lives of the people who we are trying to touch?

The reality is, yes and yes!

Obviously, these were unique to me at that moment in time, and yet the time I had spent in reflection gave me a new perspective on some of the realities. I was able to see beyond some of the issues and get more of a God kingdom view, and it helped me get some priorities straight.

For instance, consider the last three issues I mentioned.

- Communication in the heart language: Communicating heart to heart is a principle that is valid in any language. Oh, how we need to be relevant. There is so much boring stuff going on, and yet there is such excitement to the dynamism of the kingdom of God. I got more committed to learning the Ixil language.

- Hunger for the Word: I know that we cannot produce that hunger, and that is why prayer and the power of the Spirit need to be released. And I determined to be more of a man of the Word.
- Many places, many people, busy, busy, busy: And yet the work is done one by one! And I determined to be more intentional in my approach to people.

His power and His grace, His love, His forgiveness, His mercy, never changes and I was reminded once again: "Oh, the depth of the riches of the wisdom and knowledge of God! How unsearchable are His judgments, and his paths beyond tracing out! Who has known the mind of the Lord? Or who has been His counselor? Who has ever given to God, that God should repay them? For from Him and through Him and for Him are all things. To Him be the glory forever! Amen." (Romans 11:33-36)

Jesus said, "I am the vine; you are he branches. If you remain in Me and I in you, you will bear much fruit; apart from Me you can do nothing." John 15:5

When I read these verses, it moved me to a new level of abandonment of self and a surrender and commitment to Him. I really didn't have to remind you of all of that, did I? But midway in the book, I just thought it would be good to pause, to reflect, and to take a reality check!

CHAPTER 21

You Would Have Cried Too

The plane rides over Ixil country were so exciting, perhaps because of the exuberance of those light plane flights over our area, over our trails and footpaths, or perhaps it was because of the view of the beautiful, mountainous terrain from the air and getting a whole new perspective of Ixil country. Or could it have been the mighty wind of the Spirit of God sweeping over our countryside?

Whatever it was, it was certainly pulling at our heartstrings and tuning our hearts to a higher emotional level. It caused us to shed of a lot of tears—tears of joy, concern, and thanksgiving. Let me share with you.

Pap Ton was the official lemonade maker in one of the distant villages. He made it in a large washbasin, and it was obvious when he was at work because one hand was always cleaner than the other! He was always the first one to volunteer to carry something so that his people could hear the good news about Jesus Christ. Years ago, Pap Ton had put his faith in Jesus Christ upon hearing about Him in a schoolhouse meeting when some other missionaries had passed through his area. No one knew how old Pap Ton really was, but there he was, leading everyone else up the trail with back-breaking cargo. The day I remember so vividly is when Pap Ton had made a special effort to get to the airstrip to tell us goodbye. He did not take into consideration Bill Overhulser's special plane that gets up off the ground so quickly, and he was way down at the end of the short runway. Our plane was in the air before Pap Ton knew it. But he was making up for that distance by frantically running and waving his fool arm off. As we passed over him, I could see that frantically waving, clean, white hand and arm. Then it happened—Pap Ton's dedication, sincerity, and simplicity flashed before me, and I wept. And you would have wept, too!

On one occasion, two young girls from Ilom were flying with us. They were the daughters of Nan Cat from Ilom. They were fifteen and twelve and were ravaged from tuberculosis. We had offered to take them to hospital after their mother's anguished consent. We had to remove the seats to make room, so we were sitting back to back on the floor. One of the girls was weak from our trip to the airstrip from the village, and she sagged extra close to Elaine. As we climbed out of the river valley and as the plane banked, I looked out over the green blanket of trees to the Indian village. It was then I began to think of the girls' mother. She too was sick with TB, going blind, separated from her husband, and now burdened with sadness for her two daughters. We began to cry, and you would have cried too!

A month later we visited the two girls in the national TB hospital. They were already getting better! They begged us to sing some hymns, and we did. The next thing we knew, three wards of women were gathered around the pila. Some had come to wash their dishes and began singing. Some were just listening, and all had a glistening in their eyes. That day remains etched on my heart. It was one of those mystical, magical moments where the atmosphere is charged and there is a presence and a recognition that someone cares. Before it was over, we had a regular church service there in the hospital plaza around the pila. I have been in a lot of church services since then, but that had to be one of the greatest that I have ever experienced. As we were leaving, we noticed there was another glistening in the girls' and women's eyes that seemed to change to a sparkle. You would have cried too.

Then there were all the baptisms. If you would have known the lifestyles of all the men and women who stepped down into the water and then seen as they came up and out that testimony of obedience and confirmation of their faith in Jesus Christ, you would have known, beyond a shadow of a doubt, that our God is still in the business of performing miracles and changing lives. Tears were mingled with the baptismal waters—tears of joy and celebration and gratitude. It was like the early New Testament churches. Here are some of the words for those people.

> "We also thank God continually because, when you received the Word of God, which you heard from us, you accepted in not as the word of men, but as it actually is, the Word of God, which is at work in you who believe." (1 Thessalonians 2:13)

> "But you are a chosen people, a royal priesthood, a holy nation, God's special possession, that you may declare the praises of Him who called you out of darkness into his wonderful light. Once you were not a people, but now you are the people of God; once you had not received mercy, but now you have received mercy." (1Peter 2: 9-10i)

In reality, isn't this the story also of those of us who believe? Isn't it the story of we who have received the Word of God as it is and have experienced its power? Our God brought us out of darkness into His marvelous light.

> "As for us, we were dead in our transgressions and sins, in which we used to live when we followed the

> ways of this world and the ruler of the kingdom of the air, the spirit who is at work in those who are disobedient. All of us lived like that at one time, gratifying the cravings of our sinful nature and following its desires and thoughts. Like the rest, we were by nature objects of wrath. *But* because of His great love for us, God, who is rich in mercy, made us alive with Christ even when we were dead in transgressions—it is by grace we have been saved. And God raised us up with Christ and seated us with Him in the heavenly realms in Christ Jesus, in order that in the coming ages He might show the incomparable riches of His grace, expressed in His kindness to us in Christ Jesus." (Ephesians 2:1–7 emphasis added)

The drops of miracles keep coming.
Have you cried lately? Weep with us!

> "A time to weep and a time to laugh, A time to mourn and a time to dance." (Eccles. 3: 4)

> "Those who sow tears shall reap joy. Yes, they go out weeping, carrying seed for sowing, and return singing, carrying their *overflowing harvest baskets.*" (Ps. 126:5–6, emphasis added)

CHAPTER 22

We Reach the Clouds

We were headed for Vi'calama' the village at the highest elevation of one of our congregations in the Ixil area. It is comparable to Palop, but instead of being nestled in the rugged terrain, it stands more open on the mountaintop. The people who live there raise sheep, potatoes, and some corn.

Getting to Vi'calama' is a challenge. As I climbed the trail to the top where the village lies, I encountered the mist and the cold. Then at times, there was a brisk wind and rain. I had been on the trail for seven hours, and the last three hours were a tough climb up switchbacks. (It seemed to go straight up to me.) When I paused, my perspiring body quickly chilled. So it is a small wonder that the drink of hot coffee with the hot chili was so refreshing as it warmed me up. There was a reception committee waiting for me to escort me the last hour, and part of the reception was the coffee! They know how to make a guy feel good. After a day on the trail, the fellowship and the supper of meat broth and tortillas around the fire in the kitchen and dining room were out of this world.

Restful sleep on the pine needles was so refreshing for my exhausted body and mind. It rained all night along with high winds, so I was awakened many times. The corrugated tin roof on the chapel building made the sound of the torrential rain and howling wind more scandalous. (I didn't say how long of a time on the pine needles was needed!) The 7:00 a.m. starting time for the service was moved to 11:00 a.m. because of the weather. The service started, and it was a special affair because of the closing of the vacation Bible school. In fact, there were many special events, and the service ended at about two thirty. Then we had a session with the elders of the church, and the next thing I knew it was dark. We had another meal at six with more broth and tortillas, and it was still out of this world.

Ah, sweet, deep sleep on pine needles was again the order of the night. It was great. But there was the sneaky, creepy mountaintop cold that I felt in my sleeping bag at one in the morning, at three o'clock it was really taking control, and at six o'clock I abandoned the fight. I needed to be getting up anyway; I was reminded of my night in Palop.

It was dawn, and it was brilliant. It was one of those days. The time was an hour ahead of the villages in the valleys. Those long-distant low shadows were being etched across the valleys in the remote distance. What a display was before me—it almost seemed I could see forever. Then, I recalled all that had happened the day before. A place that had been void of singing, the presence of God's Word, and hope and wonder had been transformed into a splendor of adoration, and the people filled the air with the joyful noise of the love and grace of God. Thirty-seven young voices were singing, reciting scripture, and sharing testimonies of God's grace and love. A strange, good warmth came over me, and I felt the presence of God the Father. I was standing on the spot where, over a year ago, I got the news that my leader and mentor, Bill Hays, had passed on to glory. On that mountaintop, I breathed out a prayer of thanksgiving and shouted, "Hallelujah! Bill is in glory, and Jesus's kingdom marches on!"

My mind drifts back to that night when I received the news about Bill Hays. I was in the same chapel building, and it must have been about one o'clock in the morning. I was nestled in my pine needle bed when I heard a loud banging on the door. *Who could it be at this hour?* I wondered. I got up and opened the door, and there stood three Ixil men. One worked for doña Chavela, the widow of don Pedro. She had heard the news on the radio that Bill had passed, and she knew that Elaine and I would want to be at the funeral. And because of the culture, he would be buried the very next day. So she gathered some horses together; called Las (Francisco), her number-one worker, into service with two others; and sent them to bring us home. We would have never made it home in time without them. The day before, we had traveled through a terrible storm on the trail. As we traveled the same trail with Las and his men in the dark and in the early morning hours, we encountered a lot of fallen trees. It took us a lot longer to get home that time, and those three guys did a lot of chopping with their machetes. It was almost noon when we arrived. We hurriedly packed, and off we went with doña Chavela to the funeral service four hours away. We arrived in time, and we would not have wanted to miss that celebration of the life and faith of Bill. Thanks to doña Chavela and all of her efforts and those of the three men, we were able to make that unforgettable trip.

Again, my mind drifts back to even a few years earlier. My colleague Gale Morris and I were in this village around Christmastime, and we had the privilege to share the Christmas story with the new congregation. I had the flannel graph figures and the board all ready to go. I thought we would basically tell the story to the young people during the service, so we had all the young people come up front. That meant that they left their families and come down the aisles to the front platform. They sat and huddled in front of me. I began to tell and display the sacred event of the birth of Jesus. As I moved along in the story, I discovered that the older folks had gotten up and come toward the front as well. They had in reality begun to stand in front of the children. As I looked up at those standing there, it seemed as if they were spellbound. I continued to walk through the graphic form and that simplistic story of the birth of Jesus that seemed to grip everyone. It was an evening atmosphere bathed in reverence.

Gale remarked to me later, "It seemed as if they were hearing the story for the first time." Then, the thought came to me, and I said, "You know what, I believe that many *were* hearing it for the first time!"

No wonder one feels that he has reached the clouds! What a glorious privilege we had.

What drops of miracles!

CHAPTER 23

Out of the Mouths of Babes

I have a few thoughts and stories that I would like to share. I wanted to try to put into perspective the simplicity of belief and trust. I have chosen a few stories from some children that I have known to help set the stage.

While we were ministering in Guatemala, we had the opportunity to come to the States to share our ministry with the churches. We call that a furlough or deputation time. It was a time to share with our prayer partners and supporters. It involved a lot of travel and, many times, separation from our family. One time, however, I had the wonderful privilege to be able to take my family with me, and we were able to share as a family the ministry in which we were involved in Ixil country. It was so great to have my family with me because their input enhanced the programs that we presented. We were able to present various facets our ministry. We put together a few skits and dramas to help illustrate our ministry, and we all donned Ixil Mayan clothing—yes, the whole regalia. One of the outreaches we presented was the medical ministry. My son, Donnie, was old enough to carry his sister in one of those makeshift stretchers made out of a chair and a tumpline. He would carry Pamela onto the stage and set her in front of us as a very sick person who needed desperate help. This would illustrate our goal to share God's love not just with words but with actions. Obviously, there were some shaky, bumpy rides for Pam and lots of ad-libbed conversation about how sick she was. They came through like real troupers. The medical ministry played a great role in opening up many opportunities to share Jesus and His love.

We also included some cultural customs. In one of the presentations, we had the courting scene, where a young Ixil girl had her shawl (*reboso* or *ixb'u'j*) tossed over her shoulder. It was about eight feet long, and it became somewhat like a telephone line. As she would walk by a young boy, he would reach out and pull on her shawl. If she was interested, she would let the shawl be pulled off, and she would lightly tug on it to get it back. Then the two of them would playfully pull it back and forth as they talked. If she was not interested, she would yank the shawl right out of his hand. We included a few other customs, and as I said, it certainly enhanced our program. The courting one, however, really caught the attention of the younger people, and I could tell that the adults were intrigued too! We could not have done it without the younger generation.

I believe that one night the children were exhausted from all of the nightly and weekend performances because they threw me a curve. As we were coming up the back stairway of the church to walk onto the platform, I noticed that the kids weren't keeping up. After a few more steps up, I looked back and said, "Hurry up. We are on in a few minutes." I got a strange look from my oldest son, and he said, "We are not going to perform tonight!" I could hardly believe my ears. I was caught in a dire predicament on the back stairway of this church as the congregation was waiting for our entrance. Somehow US culture had caught up to us, and my kids were on strike. I had no strike buster by my side, so I pulled out a special trump card. I said, "If you will go through this program tonight, right after we're finished, we will go out for ice cream—double decker stuff!" Strike over! You just never know what ice cream can do!

Sometimes our program extended longer than the allotted time. And being that my children had heard many of the stories over and over again, I am sure that wore on their patience. I usually tried to end the program with a question-and-answer time, which often extended the program even more. One night as I was finishing up, I asked, "Are there any more questions?" Immediately, my son Paul blurted out loud and clear, "No! No, there are no more questions!"

Paul also got into the sports culture at a very early age. Near the end of some of the services and the programs, he would stand in the back and indicate that time was up with the "time out" sign. I knew it was time for me to stop. Nothing like having the kids to keep you in line!

Another time, I was involved in the migrant ministry in West Chester, Pennsylvania. One day, one of the members of the board shared a story with us. Her daughter had been invited by her friend to spend an evening at her home and share a meal with them. When her friend's family sat down to eat the meal together, they did not take a moment to pray or whatever their custom might have been before they began the meal. As soon as they started the meal, our board member shared that her daughter spoke up and said, "I don't know how it is at your house, but at our house we always thank the Lord for the food and for the time we can share together." The friend's mother couldn't wait to call our board member to share with her what had happened. The mother said that she was somewhat taken aback but was delightfully surprised. She went on to share that they would likely change their family's approach to mealtime from then on.

I shared the story with my family. And wouldn't you know, a few days later in the middle of a hectic schedule, we sat down to eat dinner and didn't even make an attempt to give thanks before diving right in. Well, it didn't take Paul very long to announce in a sanctimonious tone, "I don't know how it is at your house, but at my house, we always pause to give thanks."

One day at our Bible camp in the Poconos, I had the privilege of sharing with some young people about our adventures in Guatemala. I was telling them about Pedro, a young lad about thirteen or fourteen years old who came to the house one day because he was sick, and he told me his father did not believe him. His father told me later that he needed Pedro to stay home and work in the fields. A few days later, Pedro rode up to the house again and begged me to take him to the hospital. Well, I went off to talk to his father again, and this time, he said, "I'll let him go. Yes, he is sick, and he needs help to get better." I took Pedro off to the hospital, and the good news was that Pedro got better and came home a new young man. Then I asked the kids if they ever had a case where their parents or another adult did not believe them. One little girl shot up her hand and said, "One day I was really sick, and my mother did not believe me, so I went right up to my mother and threw up in front of her!" Well, I guess Mom became a believer.

A first-grader who was reluctant to go to school in Nebaj told her mother, "Mommy, I'm scared! I get to the corner of the schoolyard, and I just don't want to go any farther; that's why I come back home crying—I'm scared." She continued on, "But, you know what, Mommy? Those friends of mine have parents that are followers of Jesus. They tell me that their parents, our neighbors, pray every morning for strength and help and courage for them, and they don't seem to be afraid like I am. Mommy, will you pray for me that the Lord Jesus will help me?" And that mother started to pray. Later, that little girl told us that she had a new sense of help and courage and that she wasn't afraid to go to school anymore. It was through that experience that the whole family started to listen to what God's Word says about the power of Jesus.

One seven-year-old boy in our town of Nebaj said to his dad, "Dad, Jesus came to our house last night! The believers, you know those followers of Jesus, brought Him here."

"Oh, yeah," retorted the dad. "What did he look like?"

The smiling young boy replied, "Well, I don't know what He looked like, but I do know that He stayed here because He came into my heart and into Mommy's heart."

Dad had no answer for that, and from that day on this rather hard-hearted young father began to listen to the good news about Jesus and God's love.

The school principal in our town school had been unduly severe in his prejudices and treatment and punishment of a young follower of Jesus. The young girl's parents were very upset and indignant. But the little girl, without any prompting, anonymously enrolled her school principal in a correspondence course about Jesus and His love. She said, "If the principal was a follower of Jesus, he would not treat me like he does."

A young boy who lived a few houses down from us in Nebaj shared with us that his father, Juan, had been sick for months. Juan had made a confession of faith in Christ, but because there had been no real improvement in his health, the family decided to call for an aunt from the capital city. The aunt was a professional in spirit worship and all of its ramifications. The little boy said, "Boy, was I scared when she prayed. There must have been at least three bad guys moving around in the room!"

That last story did not end very happily. Juan's last days were spent in real agony, and we attended his sad funeral.

These short stories reminded us again of why we were in Guatemala. There is a very real world out there in the spiritual realm no matter what age or phase of life you are in. The Holy Word puts it like this:

> "Finally, be strong in the Lord and in His mighty power. Put on the full armor of God so that you can take your stand against the devil's schemes. For our struggle is not against flesh and blood, but against the rulers, against the authorities, against the

> powers of this dark world and against the spiritual forces of evil in the heavenly realms. Therefore put on the full armor of God so that when that day of evil comes, you may be able to stand your ground, and after you have done everything, to stand. Stand firm then, with the belt of truth buckled round your waist, with the breastplate of righteousness in place, and with your feet fitted with the readiness that comes from the gospel of peace. In addition to all this, take up the shield of faith, with which you can extinguish all the flaming arrows of the evil one. Take the helmet of salvation and the sword of the Spirit, which is the Word of God. And pray in the Spirit on all occasions with all kinds of prayers and requests. With this in mind be alert and always keep on praying for all the Lord's people." (Ephesians 6:10–18)

We need to be constantly aware of the stakes that are involved. Our prayer has been that the Spirit of God might constantly remind us of our responsibilities and our opportunities no matter where we are. It is also a reminder to be very thankful for the Father's great canopy of protection over us. There was a constant need to be reminded of the vital role of prayer in our lives.

When our daughter Pam was at boarding school, she was in a prayer group with other schoolmates. I guess she was in about the fifth or sixth grade when this occurred. The group of girls really did a lot of praying. On a couple of occasions during our visits to the school, I casually dropped off a few prayer items to them. As the days went by, I discovered that the prayer concerns were answered! I began to drop more prayer concerns off, and it got to the point that when I had a special need, I almost felt like driving the three or four hours over to the school to leave the prayer concern with them. I began to wonder, *What is the difference between them and my prayers and prayer time?* The Holy Spirit gave me the answer when He led me to this passage. I am sure you will recall the story of Jesus and the little children. "The people were bringing little children to Jesus for Him to place His hands on them, but the disciples rebuked them. When Jesus saw this, He was indignant. He said to them, 'let the little children come to Me, and do not hinder them, for the kingdom of God belongs to such as these. Truly I tell you, anyone who will not receive the kingdom of God like a little child will never enter it.' And he took the children in His arms, placed his hands on them and blessed them." (Mark 10:13-16)

So I believe the lesson is sincerity, no pretense, and simplistic faith.

Believe me, observing those young girls impacted my life. My prayer life changed—and I am still learning! So I have tried to put into practice an unpretentious, uncomplicated, simplistic (childlike!) approach. I have tried to move into a mode of "praying without ceasing" and approaching that throne of grace boldly. I believe that's why we call Him our Father!

Jesus on various occasions referred to the disciples as "little faith ones." I am sure He has referred to me as a "little faith one" too. It makes me respond to the call of, "Oh, come on! Grow up!"

And what was that all about? Summed up in a few words, never underestimate the sensitivity, insight, wisdom, and power of youth. They are not the little faith ones but little ones with a simplistic, awesome faith. And I continue to ask to have my faith increased because, when I grow up, I want to have a faith just like theirs.

I would like to share one more experience about prayer. The Briggs & Stratton engine on the light plant could be temperamental at times. As I mentioned before we became very efficient in taking it apart and putting it back together again to keep it running. There were occasions, however, when an energy crisis was out of our control. I remember one evening when we were on one of the coffee plantations close to the village of Ilom. The motor would not start. I pulled and pulled on the starter rope and I tried all my tweaking for any idiosyncrasies—no avail. Darkness was falling and a crowd was gathering. Bill Overhulser, the pilot who had flown us in with his plane, had decided to spend the night with us on the plantation. He came up alongside of me and said, "Try it again." I looked at him in disbelief. But, after his insistence, I yanked on the cord one more time. Rrrr —off it started to run! I asked Bill, "What did you do?" He replied that he had gone into one of the plantation's empty rooms and talked to the Father about the engine— "a drop of a miracle!". And the Jesus Film began to thread through the projector's sprocket and showed brightly on the stretched sheet. There is no energy crisis with the Father!

It is no wonder the early disciples appealed to Jesus: "Teach us to pray" (Luke 11:1)

CHAPTER 24

Happiness

In a recent *Houston Chronicle*, on the comics page, *Argyle Sweaters* had a little blurb of life's unanswered questions: Actually, it was a panel with some frames depicting some of those mysteries. One of the frames had a signpost with a directional bar that was pointing to the west with the inscription; *Happiness 5 miles.*

Really, is happiness only five miles down the road?

Along this journey of faith that you and I are making, we are the recipients of the drops of miracles. Jesus dispenses them as if there were an inexhaustible supply. He is also the dispenser of joy and happiness. Yes, I know that there is a difference between joy and happiness. However, in the 1970s, we were caught up in this happiness bit.

- Happiness is to have a full tank of gas.
- Happiness is seeing dry roads after driving through two days of an ice storm in Tennessee and Arkansas. The roads were unbelievably slick.
- Happiness is to have an extra spare on the roof when you just had a flat tire in one of those desolate, lonely desert spots in Mexico.

- Happiness is being close to returning back home and hearing the children cheer when they saw the road signs heralding the Guatemalan border.
- Happiness is seeing the excitement of our children with their reunion with their boarding school friends.
- Happiness is seeing the sun again after five days of rain, drizzle, mist, and heavy cloud cover. We thought it would be the dry season by now.
- Happiness is to know that all of those wonderful friends that we made and that we were reacquainted with that past year are praying more intensely for us.
- Happiness is to know that there are those who are deeply interested and committed to getting the ambulance to the Ixil people.
- Happiness is seeing Elaine getting her color back and her strength back after nine long days of dysentery and fever.
- Happiness is to know that there is no energy crisis with God our Father.
- Happiness is to know that the kingdom of God and the church marches on without Don Lawrence.

These notes were taken after we had returned to Guatemala after a year in the States. Let me elaborate on a few of the points.

When we were at the point in time when we were to return to Guatemala, I was thinking that happiness was a full tank of gas. Our journey started in Maryland during the day of the energy crisis of 1979. One day, cars with odd-numbered license plates got to fill up, and the next day, those with even-numbered plates got to fill up. It was the time of flags waving in front of the gas stations; a green flag meant, yes, we have gas, while a red flag meant don't bother to pull in. We had a long drive in front of us—across the States to the US–Mexico border and then through Mexico to Guatemala. Would you believe that as we traveled through the United States, each time we needed gas we found a green flag flapping in the wind? It was almost as if someone was going on ahead of us arranging the whole thing. Then there was Mexico. They seemed to have plenty of gas. It was the border area that was the problem. People from the States were crossing over and filling up, so the Mexican and US authorities were cracking down. I had watched that gas gauge needle, and as we approached the border it was shivering a hair above "E". I had coaxed it along because we knew there was plenty of gas across the border and, another plus, it was cheaper too! We had not heard that much about the crackdown on the fill-ups across the border. When we finally got through the border crossing, I pulled into the first gas station. The attendants came running out saying, "No way! No gas." Just then, over by another set of pumps, someone called out, "Go ahead and fill them up. They are okay!" That someone, of all people, was a Guatemalan truck driver who was hauling things to Guatemala and had overheard the gas station attendants talking to us. I guess he had stopped there many times before because he got their attention and they gave us the gas. He said he noticed our Guatemalan license plate and decided to help us out. Yes, happiness is a full tank of gas! And isn't it wonderful to know that there is no energy crisis with Jesus?

Happiness is seeing dry roads after driving for two days through an unbelievable ice storm in Tennessee and Arkansas. What a scary experience that was, and to make matters worse I had loaded our Chevy Suburban to the brim. Before we left that last night, I got a stepladder and piled more stuff on top of what I had already packed on the roof rack. So, right from the start even on a good road, the car seemed a little off balance. With everything coated with ice, the difficulty I had controlling the car was magnified. It just seemed to be swaying way too much. I sat in a constant rigid position, always trying to compensate and fearing that I would overreact and overcompensate and send us into a skid. I also was very vocal. About every few minutes, I would shout that everyone should stay seated—don't move! Can you imagine those young children sitting still for two days? As I pulled out of the gas station on the evening of that second day close to the Texas border, I noticed something different about the road surface. I guess I drove about a quarter of a mile before processing that the road was bare and dry. Then it dawned on me! I pulled over to the side on of the road, got out of the car, put my hands palms down on the road, and in a worshipful posture thanked God for a clear highway. The kids say I actually kissed the road! Maybe I did, but I bet they did too.

We know that happiness, real happiness, is having Jesus Christ live in our hearts and direct our lives every moment of every day. And yes, having the joy of the Lord as our strength on that journey changes the happiness quotient to the joy quotient! We realize that real joy does not depend on outward circumstances and that it is the change from being just happy to having the Spirit's special fruit—joy. Of course, it is nice to have an extra spare on the roof, an extra parachute, a full tank of gas, a clear bare road and stability for your load, but those are not things that bring deep, lasting contentment. No, we do not depend on these kinds of things to fill our happiness quotient. It goes much deeper than that. It is the fullness of God's Holy Spirit that brings full and overflowing contentment no matter the circumstances or situations. Paul caught the mystical nature of the moment when he wrote,

> "Rejoice in the Lord always. I will say it again: Rejoice! … for I have learned to be content whatever the circumstances. I know what it is to be in need, and in what it is to have plenty I have learned the secret of being content, whether well fed or hungry, whether living in plenty or in want. I can do all things through Christ Jesus who gives me strength." (Philippians 4:4, 11–13)

Toward the end of Paul's letter to the believers in the church at Rome, he interjects a prayer. His letter to the believers is filled with such powerful God talk that it seems he takes a moment to catch his breath close to the end and says, "May the God of hope fill you with all joy and peace as you trust in Him, so you may overflow with hope by the power of the Holy Spirit" (Romans 15:13).

Paul picks the two most elusive, sought-after, emotional entities to zero in our focus—peace and joy. He emphasizes not just some joy but all joy, and full and abundant joy at that. Then he tacks on the "so that you may overflow with hope." You see, hope powered by the Holy Spirit crowns joy and peace. Because if you have the great hope that Paul talks about in this letter to the church in Rome, you will have gifted to you out of the bag of grace everything you need for a fulfilled journey with Jesus.

How is your happiness quantity? Have you discovered the secret? And can you declare with Paul that you are content and can do all things through Christ Jesus who gives you strength? Do you hold in your hand the super trump card of hope? Are you filled with all joy?

This kind of hope we are talking about is not the "once upon a time" myth or legend, the last-one-out-of-Pandora's-box kind of thing. No, our hope is the genuine, authentic, real deal. It is based on the reality of the One who never fails and always fulfills what He promises to do. This hope cuts through the anxieties and dissipates the fog and waves of fear and disbelief. Phillips Brooks got it right when he wrote the line, "The hopes and fears of all the years are met in Thee tonight" ("O Little Town of Bethlehem"). Jesus is the Way, the Truth, and the Life, and He is also the hope. He is hope personified.

Isn't it interesting that we began in the search for happiness and became immersed in hope? I am convinced that if you have Jesus, you have everything you need for your spiritual journey in the kingdom! As I mentioned earlier, out of that bag of grace you and I get great hope. Yes, when Jesus came, He came to unlock the divine splendor that is in each one of us. And one of the things He unleashed was our great hope. If you have this hope, you will never be disillusioned or disappointed.

Missionary pilot Don Donaldson had a logo over the instrument panel in the cockpit of his plane that read, "This engine may fail, but Jesus never fails."

Jesus never fails!

Out of this hope springs peace and joy. And if joy is peace dancing, there is surrounding you and me a jubilant crowd. They are surrounding us in jubilation in an uninhibited, endless victory dance. Let's join in, and we won't let fear and disbelief cut in and get carried away dancing to another tune!

Got joy? I hope so—wait, no, no—I *know* with great expectation and anticipation. I know you have joy!

CHAPTER 25

You Are in the Army Now

Francisco went to town on market day. He was the eighteen-year-old son of one of our church members in an outlying village. Our Sunday market day was the largest in Ixil country, and Ixil people from all over the area came to it. It was a great day to get all your supplies for the rest of the week. It was also a good day for a young man to catch up on all the happenings in Ixil country. This particular Sunday was a good day for the Guatemalan army to draft young men. The civil war was escalating, and these were turbulent times, so the Guatemalan army and the government were trying to get a handle on the instability by drafting young men throughout the country. Francisco did not know that this market day on this Sunday was also draft day. The army drafted quite a few men on that day, Francisco included. Fortunately (or unfortunately), Francisco had his identification papers with him, so he did not have to go back home to get them—a six-hour-walk away. The next thing Francisco knew, he was in the army and off to boot camp.

When Francisco's parents and grandmother found out that he was gone, they were distraught. They came immediately to the house and appealed to me, and I took them to the town hall and spoke to the mayor. The mayor and the town hall officials told us it was completely out of their hands now that the government had drafted him. The grandmother was distressed. "How can we get him back?" she asked. "Well," they said, "there is a way of appeals that could be made, especially on the grandmother's part, and she could say that she is completely dependent on her grandson."

So we began the process of the paperwork, the official documents, and the visits to the army officials. During the process, the father wanted to visit his son. One day I took the father and his companion to the capital city to go visit his son on a base that was in the southern part of Guatemala. I went to the capital's central bus terminal, where riders could catch a bus to almost anywhere. I found the bus that went right past the base. I put the two men on the bus and turned them over to the driver and the helper who said that they would make sure they got off at the right spot. I felt reassured that they were in good hands, and I reassured Francisco's father with the same feeling. I returned to my car and felt pretty good about leaving them in the good hands of the driver. I had not taken into consideration that this was the first time that these two men had been this far from their home. The next thing I knew, there was a knock on the car window. There they were, making an urgent appeal for me to take them to the base myself. So they got in the car and I took them to the base and got to see Francisco. He looked well and was delighted to see us. We told him we had an appeal in the works and for him to hang in there.

The process continued, and things looked bright for his release. One day, the father received word that we could go to the base for the final hearing for Francisco's release. When we arrived at the base, we were received and ushered into the office of the first sergeant. This was the first stop before the captain's office. We went through some introductions and the review of the paperwork. Then they called for Francisco. He came in, gave the proper salutes, and stood at rigid attention. "So," the sergeant said, "you, Private Francisco, you want to get out of the army, is that correct?"

"Oh, no, sir," replied Francisco, "I don't want to get out of the army, sir!" Well, talk about faded hope and expectations. We were breathless!

"Well," said the sergeant, "You heard what Private Francisco said. No use calling the Captain in. Case dismissed! You are dismissed, Private Francisco, to return to your duties. And for you men, have a good day and a good trip!"

Well, that ended that.

A few years later, I met Francisco in our town. He had gotten out of the army, and he said that it was the best thing that could have ever happened to him. He had learned to read, he came to know Jesus as his Savior and Lord, and he now had a job as a teacher in one of the villages in Ixil country. His grandmother was still living and was happy.

So Romans 8:28 still rings true: "And we know that in all things God works for the good of those who love Him, who had been called according to His purpose."

I call the pearl-handled .45 another part of the story of "You Are in the Army Now." As I have mentioned before, the army was occupying our town, so their very presence made it necessary to interact with the soldiers. One day, two young men, both sergeants, came to the house. I was not really sure what they were up to until they asked me if I could give them some English classes. I said I would be delighted to. I thought it would be a great opportunity to reach some of the soldiers with the Word of God. We began the classes in my office that was in our house. I was using some English as a second language (ESL) materials and also the Gospel of John as a textbook. One night as we were reading the Gospel of John, one of the sergeants, who was also named John (Juan), fell under great conviction. I told him to not hesitate but to be open to what the Holy Spirit was dealing with him about. Juan said, "I could never be accepted by God because of what this has done," as he slumped his head on my desk and patted his pearl-handled .45 that was tucked in the holster on his side

"Oh, no, Juan," I said. "This is just what our Father delights to do—to call His child back to Himself. Nothing, no nothing, can ever keep Him from accepting you. Listen to what Saint Paul has to say:

> "I thank Christ Jesus our Lord, who has given me strength, that He considered me trustworthy, appointing me to His service. Even though I was once a blasphemer and a persecutor and a violent man, I was shown mercy because I acted in ignorance and unbelief. The grace of our Lord was poured out on me abundantly, along with the faith and love that are in Christ Jesus.
>
> Here is a trustworthy saying that deserves full acceptance: Christ Jesus came into the world to save sinners — of whom I am the worst. But for that very reason I was shown mercy so that in me, the worst of the sinners, Christ Jesus might display his immense patience as an example for those who would believe in Him and receive eternal life. Now to the King eternal, immortal, invisible, the only God, be honor and glory for ever and ever. Amen.'"
> (1Timothy 1: 12- 17)

That night Juan gave his heart to Christ. He was a good musician and began to attend our church. He could play the guitar and would lead us in worship music. Very soon he began to receive opposition from his superiors in the army. In fact, one day, he was told to quit playing and singing those gospel songs. Juan couldn't stop doing that, so they tore up his songbook. He told me later that it did not matter; he had all the songs memorized anyway. A short time later,

Juan was transferred, and I didn't hear from him for a while. Then one day I met someone who knew him and said that he had gotten out of the army. He was now traveling the countryside playing, singing, and repairing musical instruments in the churches.

One never knows what wonderful results will happen when the Word of God is coupled with the Holy Spirit and set loose in power. Praise God from whom all blessings flow and for drops of a miracle cascading down on Francisco and Juan. Yes, praise God! Amen and amen!

CHAPTER 26

Dark Night of the Soul

Have you ever had a dark night of the soul? Thomas did, and out of the darkness of his doubts he said, "Unless I see the nail marks in His hands and put my finger where the nails were, and put my hand into His side, I won't believe it!" (John 20:25). Peter had one of those dark nights when he denied Jesus and his soul was struck with such remorse that he wept bitterly (Mark 14:66–72). Even Paul, who was the ever-positive crusader, hints at his dark night and the loss of peace of mind. He gives us a long list of his "adventures" in his second letter to the Corinthians (2 Corinthians 11:21–33). It would be hard to imagine that he did not have an episode of the dark night after being exposed to such turmoil. He shared in the first part of the letter to the Corinthians a hint of that kind of experience when he said, "For when we came to Macedonia, we had no rest, but we were harassed at every turn—conflicts on the outside, fears within. But God, who comforts the downcast, comforted us by the coming of Titus, and not only by his coming but also the comfort you had given him" (2 Corinthians 1:5–7).

So, we are in good company, and I can remember one vivid night. I had been struggling with the thoughts about my call to Guatemala. Some disappointments and discouragement helped foster the feelings. Finally, it came to a point of frustration, and

I began to question the validity of my being in Ixil country. Why did it seem to be so hard? Had I just worked up this "missionary endeavor"? Was I really supposed to be here? I was getting the oppressive feeling of depression. What was I to do?

During this brooding sense of frustration, I recalled a conversation that I had with my pastor Jim Tarr years ago. Pastor Jim and his wife, Jean, had been associated with a dark night of the soul during their journey with Jesus. They were both qualified to share about calling, belief, and doubt. Jean had been diagnosed with a brain tumor, and the twilight of doubt that crept into their lives at that point was turning into a murky darkness. They felt the extreme urge that they had to know! Know what? They had to know that this was not just something that happened but that somehow, in all of this, the Father had a purpose—not to explain at that moment but to reassure that He is true to His word.

Pastor Jim said, "We pulled ourselves together and went out the back door of the house into the backyard. We then just completely abandoned themselves in total surrender to the Father and cried out, 'We have just got to know!' And do you know what? We found out! He let us know. Oh, what a wonderful moment of assurance that was. We felt enveloped in an atmosphere of love and mercy and holiness and purpose. Our hearts were bathed in calm assurance. Yes, He will let you know!"

I rehearsed that conversation and played it through my mind and heart. It spurred me on to realize that I, too, had to know! I went out the front door with that mind-set. I went out into a typical Nebaj evening. I began to walk in the drizzle and mist and wondered where to go to get this darkness consumed by the divine splendor. I just had to know—*Am I to be here in Ixil country? There seem to be such meager results. And what about my call?*

Not many people were out that night, and the next thing I knew I was at the steps of the Catholic church. I climbed the steps, and when I entered, it felt a little unsettling. There were two feeble twenty-five-watt light bulbs struggling to illuminate the vast area.

Candles burned at the front and cast an eerie glow. There were some kneeling faithful parishioners reciting prayers and an Ixil shaman chanting rather loudly. Incense drifted and enveloped me. I walked to a darkened, secluded corner in the foyer. "I need to know!" I cried. Then, the Father who knows our hearts answered! Almost as dramatically as my beach experience, He showed up! Just as sure and clear, it came.

He took me to the parable of the sower. I want to take the liberty to share this familiar parable with you from Matthew's gospel:

> "A farmer went out to sow his seed. As he was scattering the seed, some fell along the path, and the birds came and ate it up. Some fell on rocky places, where it did not have much soil. It sprang up quickly, because the soil was shallow. But when the sun came up, the plants were scorched, and they withered because they had no root. Other seed fell among thorns, which grew up and chocked the plants. Still other seed fell on good soil, where it produced a crop—a hundred, sixty or thirty times what was sown. Whoever has ears, let him hear." (Matthew 13:3–8)

When He finished, He said, "Now, go! Go and keep sowing and leave the results to Me!"

"Okay," I said. "Enough—now I know!"

That is what He said: "You will seek me and find me when you seek me with all your heart" (Jeremiah 29:13 NIV).

CHAPTER 27

The Word

Have you ever stopped for a moment to think how blessed we are to have the Bible right at our fingertips? Not just that we can turn the pages, but also in the technological, digital sense, with our tablets and smart phones. And we have so many different versions to choose from, we seem to be inundated. With that in mind, it is almost impossible to think about people who do not or did not have that kind of blessing available. We are surrounded by so many books and so much technology, it is difficult to appreciate areas in the world where people are without those benefits. Well, not too long ago and not that far away, I was awakened to some of those realities.

One Sunday morning in the plaza, I was rejoicing in the fact that now there were ample copies of the Gospel of Mark available in the Ixil language. Thanks to the dedicated efforts of the Wycliff Translators, Ray and Helen Elliott, I was able to share this drop of a miracle. I had taken advantage of the Sunday market day to set up a table in the busy town square plaza and share the good news about God's love. About midday an elderly Ixil day man stopped by our small table. I read a short portion to him from Mark's Gospel, and as I read I showed him how to follow along. He listened intently, and I was encouraged, so I said to him, "Isn't it wonderful? Just think—God's Word in your own language!" But he replied to me,

"No, no, this could never be God's Word to me. Bah! God's Word! That is a lie. What did you do—grab a hold of God's hand and say, 'Come write this down for me'? That is a lie, what you say!" Then he glared at me with that perturbed, penetrating, quizzical look that said, *What do you take me for?* Then he turned and stomped away through the crowd with the nod of approval of his countrymen.

I tried to imagine why this elderly man would say this, and I reflected on his situation. This was possibly the first time he had ever seen his language written down. He could not read or write, nor could he understand very much of the trade language, Spanish. His wife could not read or write and understood even less than he did of Spanish. His son and daughter-in-law could not read or write. His small grandson had been off to a Spanish-speaking school for two years and was not making much progress. So, for all practical purposes, they were monolingual. Then what was God's Word to these people? Where does God's Word come from? Who had the authority and the holiness and power to handle God's Word? Well, if it is not written, then it must be oral. My grandfather had heard it and abided by it, and my mother and father had followed it and it was good enough for them. So that is the way it is! "God's Word" comes through oral tradition. So who handles God's Word? There has to be someone or some people "in charge." Someone must be keeping track of it, right? And there is—there was (and is) a whole array of religious practitioners. There are "day counters," and there were those that keep the account straight in the spiritual realm. There were those that interpreted dreams. Ancestors need to be taken into account, and all other kinds of spiritual accounting were taken into consideration. And some had their ritual bags filled with objects that have spiritual power. And now, throw in the conquistadors' religion brought from Spain and you had quite a system going. It was almost like, "Oh, wow, more gods to worship!" And believe me, it worked for them. The culture was intricately tied to and woven into the spiritual realm. This spiritual element was woven into all society, customs, and culture. It touched every moment of everyday life. And there was this whole group of religious practitioners with various ranks and reputation. They were the middlemen, the go-betweens, the intermediaries and intercessors, and they had their traditional rituals in this spiritual realm. They covered from the birth to the death and all in between. Planting, washing, traveling, and that problem with your mother-in-law— "we have it covered" could be their motto. This is a very small thumbnail sketch of a very complex religious system. In short terms, this is why they have created their own god and gods that they can manipulate and placate. This is why candles and incense and the "keeping of days" could become so important. This is why it was so essential to pay some go-between to keep the account straight. This is why a piece of wood, a stone in the cornfield, a mountaintop, a dream, the stream, the wind—and on and on—could carry so much meaning. That is why fear and superstition were rampant.

And that is the reason we go!

What hope is there? "Your Word is truth."

"Heaven and earth shall pass away, but my Word shall not pass away."

"Lord to whom shall we go? You have the words of eternal life!"

So, in the final analysis, we must rest in the hope of the one true God and Father and His Word and the power of the Holy Spirit as they make known the work of Jesus the Christ.

We praise God for the dedicated people around the world who are translating God's Word into the heart languages of the people they live with. We have especially appreciated Ray and Helen Elliott's efforts in Ixil country. They dedicated their lives and their hearts into putting God's Word down in a correct, concise, complete, and understandable form in the heart language of the Ixil people. We praise God for rising up Ixil men and women who continue in the task of getting God's Word to their own people to this very day. And we praise God that there are Ixil men and women, boys and girls who have already taken God's Word for what it is and have put their faith and trust in Jesus as their Savior, Lord, and God.

To the people of Thessalonica, Paul wrote, "And, we also thank God continually because, when you received the Word of God, which you heard from us, you accepted it not as the word of men, but as it actually is, the Word of God, which is at work in you who believe" (1 Thess. 2:13). Paul prefaced this with these words about the Thessalonians:

"The Lord's message rang out from you not only in Macedonia and Achaia—your faith in God has become known everywhere. Therefore, we do not need to say anything about it, for they, themselves, report what kind of reception you gave us. They tell how you turned from idols to serve the living and true God, and to wait for his Son from heaven, whom He raised from the dead—Jesus who rescues us from the coming wrath." (1 Thessalonians 1:8–10)

That kind of message contains the wonderful news that continues to ring out throughout the world—that same message that came to those shepherds on that hillside that night so long ago: "Today in the city of David a Savior is born!" That good news echoes through the streets and villages and on the trails today. Praise God for His Word and the power of the Holy Spirit. And we humbly thank Him for the marvelous privilege to have had the opportunity to share that Word with the Ixil. What more could we have asked for than to have had a small part in His plans and purposes in the advancement of the kingdom? Amen!

CHAPTER 28

Throw Your Sombrero in the Air

I met him on the trail as he was coming back from one of his evangelical thrusts into Ixil villages in Ixil country. There wasn't enough money to pay him for what he did; he was always on the move, always sharing Jesus. Sometimes it seemed that he wasn't real. He was human all right, right down to the core, and he was embodied with the gift of evangelism. Luis had that special one-to-one relationship that just had to be a gift of the Spirit. He was not a polished preacher, but my, how he could share God's Word with individuals. That gift propelled Luis to penetrate many Ixil villages for Christ Jesus. Luis was our Ixil evangelist.

In fact, on a few occasions, Luis took our visions and talks into the world of accomplished reality. While we sat around talking, Luis did the walking. He was the one who penetrated a village that we had prayed about for years.

I can remember sitting on a mountainside that had a great view into a valley of the distant western border of Ixil country. I asked one of the Ixil leaders when we were going to share the good news of Jesus with those in that village that we could see off in the distance.

He replied, "Oh, no, hearts are too hard in that village!"

But that was just the kind of challenge the Holy Spirit and Luis relished. Just because there were hard hearts—shucks—that did not deter Luis, let alone the Holy Spirit. Commissioned and sent by the Holy Spirit, Luis went off to that village. Yes, he went into that hard-hearted village. He began to share the claims of Jesus Christ with his countrymen. The Word of God, linked with the power of the Spirit, channeled through this humble man. It did not take long for the village to find out about their new "believer."

Let me paint a little background that makes this story pulsate even more with the continuation of the Acts of the Holy Spirit. Two incidents stand out.

One day when Luis was heading toward that village on the western slope, he met two men who were on their way to their cornfields. They recognized Luis and warned him.

"Don't go down into the village today," they said. "There are some men on the trail waiting with their machetes for you. They want to do away with you. They think you are evil. Take our advice or suffer the consequences!"

"Oh, I must go down into the village," replied Luis. "My people need to hear the good news about Jesus!" And off he went under the canopy of the Spirit.

There was also a group of strong, almost cultic, hardline, traditional Ixil Mayan spirit worshipers who related somewhat to the Catholic church. This group, which had powerful influence in the village, thought that they could get some help in preventing Luis and his visits to the village by sending an appeal to the district priest.

They sent an appeal to their local district priest, which said, "Get an order to prevent this evangelical traveling preacher from coming to our village. And if he does come, have a directive order to have him thrown in jail!"

The priest sent back the reply: "Praise God, the Word of God is coming to your village!" Now that is kingdom stuff!

Because of Luis's consistent walk and talk, the power of the

Word, and the work of the Holy Spirit, one of the men in this village put his faith in Jesus Christ. This decision did not go unnoticed, and he experienced some real pressure from his colleagues.

These colleagues and some other leaders in his village came to visit him. "Why," they asked him, "would you turn your back on the traditions and the real gods?"

They spoke with continued pressure. "You should know that there is no real god like ours in this new religion of yours. How can you forsake the things of our fathers? You are treading on dangerous ground not only with the gods and spirits but with us too! Be very, very careful!" they warned.

This man was not old in the sense that we refer to old age, but he had distinguishing gray hair about the temple. In other words, he had enough age status among his people to carry some respect. His friends came to visit, and their curiosity turned to hostility.

The man energized by the Spirit responded, "Look at me. Yes, look at me my friends," he said. "You are not talking to some child. Look at my hair and my face—they show that I carry age. It is true that I cannot read or write. Ah, how many years have you been coming to me and telling me about the gods, the spirits, the traditions, the ancestors, the accounts in the spirit world—and I listened! And how many years have I been coming to you all and telling you about the spirit gods and our beliefs and traditions—and you all listened! But, my friends, let me get one thing absolutely straight. Listen, listen—*empty* is the word and sour is its taste of what we have been feeding on! But, when our countryman Luis came to me and told me the things about God and Jesus and His love for me from the 'book,' those words passed through my ears and fell down upon my heart. They fell down as the sweetest things that I have ever heard. And now I am full!

And now, I would encourage you to listen also to the reality of the true God's love story for you and me and let those words from the 'book' pass through your ears and fall upon your heart as the sweetest thing you have ever heard. Let them fill you, and believe me, you'll never be hungry or thirsty again!"

When we heard the story, we shouted, "Throw your sombrero in the air! Because no one can work like Jesus can!"

Now, how can you just stand there with your hat still in your hand? Throw your sombrero in the air in celebration of someone coming to Jesus. Throw it in the air in celebration of the Word and the power of the Word coupled with the Holy Spirit. Throw it in the air in celebration that even though some people do not have the same shingle out in front of their church that ours has, they still appreciate and are open to the power of the Word of God. Throw your sombrero in the air that some men and women are still compelled and propelled by the Holy Spirit and that, in spite of all obstacles, they reach others for Jesus and His kingdom. Throw your sombrero in the air that some people seem to quickly reach a rich spiritual maturity in Jesus and His Word and say it like it is—"Why, those words passed through my ears and fell upon my heart as the sweetest ..."

Throw your sombrero in the air!!

CHAPTER 29

Come See Where We Live

Just the mention of the word *furlough* conjures up a whole bag of emotions. Mission boards have historically decided that it is a good idea to set aside some time to share the missionary's ministry with the sending churches. The concept is that, after serving a certain amount of time, missionaries would be granted a time frame to return to their countries and share their ministries. The amount of time spent in the field before going on furlough varied with the mission boards. Our mission board had a four-year term of service when we first went to Guatemala, but our first term of service turned out to be five years with the extra year of language school. As the years went by, the term of service for furlough became more flexible.

This furlough time included reconnecting with family and friends, perhaps engaging in some educational experiences, and, of course, visiting the churches. The sending churches were the critical link for the mission endeavor. They needed to know what an important role they played. Without the prayer support, the financial support, and the encouragement, missions would be a very weak endeavor. Perhaps they could not exist at all. The sending churches needed to hear about the missions just like they did in Saint Paul's New Testament days. The idea included that perhaps the missionaries needed a little break too. After all, their job was to work themselves out of a job.

On the missionary's side, it meant relocating the family, including a new place to live, new schools, a lot of travel, and many times separation for the family because of speaking and presentation engagements. It could be seen as a disruption, but we decided to think of it as a privilege and opportunity to have it as a part of our ministry. We felt that the mission board, the churches and the people who stood with us deserved a report and accountability from us.

In the late 1970s, it came time for us to begin a furlough. So we needed a house to serve as a base of operations. That is no little thing when you go cold calling about a residence for some months. I decided to use my network; I connected with a home church in our hometown in Maryland, the same church that got involved with the first ambulance that came to Guatemala.

We connected with Rev. Glenn Stevens, who was the pastor at the Waugh-Fork Church in Maryland. Pastor Glenn got into action right away trying to get a house for us. A young woman, Judy Mays, lived right next door to Elaine's mother and was a member of his congregation. She wanted to get involved with Pastor Glenn in pursuit of obtaining a home for us. Judy had had a dramatic conversion to Jesus Christ and was deeply committed to Jesus and His kingdom. We were glad that she was on board.

A few months went by and Pastor Glenn was delighted to inform us that they had found a house for us. It was ideal! A professor at Maryland University was going on a sabbatical to Europe for a year and was willing to rent out his house, and it fit right into our schedule. It was located very close to our hometown. With the big issue of where to live out of the way, we began our journey of deputation with peace of mind.

We flew into Florida from Guatemala and picked up a car provided by a church in Jonestown, Pennsylvania. The Jonestown church had a ministry of providing vehicles for missionaries on furlough. What a great blessing! The Primitive Methodist church in Plant City offered to put us up for a few days. We held a few meetings there, and they surprised us with a paid visit to Disney World! After our time at Plant City, we began to drive north to Maryland, where we would stay for the next year.

Somewhere in South Carolina, I stopped to give Pastor Glenn a call to see how things were going concerning the house. I was stunned when he told me that the deal was off. He said that the professor had called him and said that he was not going to Europe after all and so would not be able to rent the house. I held the phone in my hand for a few minutes trying to process what I had heard. Pastor Glenn came back on to break the silence and said not to be concerned because Judy had had a vision. Pastor Glenn and Judy had gone to pay a visit to the professor to make sure his plans would not change and see if maybe there was a possibility that the house would still be available. He assured them that the plans were final and that the house would not be available. As Pastor Glenn and Judy were leaving and crossing the front lawn, Judy stopped and suggested that they pray. After the prayer, Judy told the pastor not to worry because she had a vision of a house for Don and Elaine and it had four white pillars. When Pastor Glenn hung up, I was processing some more!

When we arrived in Maryland, Joe and Pat Morrone, Elaine's sister and brother-in-law, took us in as they had done so many times before. Judy could not pinpoint the location of the house, so we began to pursue some other leads and advertisements. Nothing—our searching ended in zero results. Then we got a call from Ruthie, the wife of my nephew Richie. She told us that the house next door to theirs was up for rent and that we should come over and look at it. We made arrangements to do so. When we pulled up in front of the house, Elaine and I remarked to each other, "I don't see any white pillars!" As we went up the front porch and the owner opened the door to let us in, there they were—four white pillars going right smack down the center of the living room! We stood there a moment to take it all in. Then the owner told us that the house used to be an old country store, and they had built a living room right around the four pillars that were on the porch. They wanted to make more living space, and it sure made a unique centerpiece.

During the process of moving in, Elaine went to her mother's home to pick up some household items, and Judy, after hearing about the house, wanted to ride along with Elaine to see it. Judy had no idea where the house was located. Elaine told me later that when they rounded a bend near the house, Judy pointed and exclaimed, "That's the house!" She didn't have to open the front door—she knew the pillars were there. (And I know what you are thinking—*Why couldn't Judy pinpoint where the house was?* Ah, the mystery and beauty of divine intervention.)

Judy had one more vision to share with us. One day when we were getting close to our return date to Guatemala, I received a telephone call from her. She said she had had another vision. I perked up and prepared to take it all in. She said that she saw us surrounded by a hedge of fire. People tried to get to us to do us harm, but the hedge of fire prevented them from touching us and even getting close.

Little did we realize that the next few years in Guatemala would be filled with such violence and danger—obviously, much more so than we anticipated. We realized that the hedge held up. On some occasions, it was very evident. What can I say?

"In the last days, God says, I will pour out my Spirit on all people. Your sons and daughters will prophesy, your young men will see visions, your old men will dream dreams. Even on my servants, both men and women, I will pour out my Spirit in those days and they will prophesy." (Acts 2:17–18)

"O Lord, open his eyes so he may see." (2 Kings 6:17)

CHAPTER 30

The Hedge of Fire

While talking about the hedge of fire, let me tell you about one day in the life of our children, Don and Pam. They were off at a boarding school five hours away in the city of Quezaltenago. Don had pestered us about getting a motorcycle, and he found one that he liked. After much negotiating with us and the owner, he became the proud owner of a Bultaco, a classic, Spanish-made, off-road, big, sturdy bike.

Don and Pam liked to get away from school at times for short visits, and we got word that they were coming for a weekend. I took my son Paul with me, and I thought we could meet them about an hour or so out of town. We got to a spot on our ridge road where it seemed we could see forever, and we decided to wait there. We could see the valley below and the plateau and the mountain ranges in the distance with the volcano peaks protruding. We waited and waited. After a few hours, twilight drifted in on us with no Don and Pam in sight, so we decided to return home.

Of course, we were wondering what had happened. Meanwhile, a strong storm came through Nebaj, so for sure we thought the trip was off.

Later that night, there was a knock at the door. It was Belisario, the telegraph operator. He told us he had a phone call from Don in Sacapulas; they were stranded in Sacapulas with motorcycle problems. Belisario also said that we were very fortunate because that was the one and only call he had been able to receive because of the storm. We thanked him and began to prepare for the hour-and-a-half trip to Sacapulas. Elaine had prepared pizzas for Don and Pam's arrival, so we put them in the Cheve Surburban and off we went.

When we arrived in Sacapulas, we found Don and Pam with some bruises, bumps, and cuts, but they were basically okay. However, they had a story to tell. The first part of the trip, an hour or so, from Quezaltenango to Huehuetenango went well. The next part led them on a road that followed the plateau above the river and then dropped down into the river valley to the town of Sacapulas. It was on this stretch of road that the EGP (*Ejercito Guerrilla de los Pobres,* the Guerrilla Army of the Poor) had decided to camp out. They were not there for a picnic. Their intention was to interrupt traffic and create terror.

Perhaps because of the innocence of youth or the complete confidence in the care of the heavenly Father, Don and Pam rode on. Perhaps they were oblivious to the stark reality that the peace, the tranquility, the stability, and the security of our area was gone! Perhaps no one had warned them. They rode on. Then, right at the wrong spot, they got a flat tire.

The Bultaco's tires were made to keep going but only with one person on the bike. So they decided that Don would go on to Sacapulas to get the tire fixed while Pam started walking. Sacapulas was about seven kilometers away (a little over four miles). Don went off, and Pam began to walk through the infestation of the EGP (just the mention of those initials struck fear into the hearts of a lot of people).

Don finally got the tire fixed and started back to get Pam. It began to get dark. Don found Pam, and they headed back to Sacapulas. But the feeble light, a flashlight rigged on the handlebars, was not enough; Don hit a boulder on the side of the road. They both somersaulted off the bike. Bad news—Pam was hurt.

Because it was so dark, they could not determine how bad Pam's injuries were. The bike was not damaged, and they hastened to get to Sacapulas for medical aid. The injuries were not serious, just a few cuts and bruises to the face. They had also heard and seen the storm on the mountain. This blow to their journey, however, forced them to suspend the trip and call us. This is where we came in. We loaded the motorcycle and the kids in the Suburban and enjoyed the pizza on the ride back home.

The next morning, we heard reports of the EGP's activities on the road that Don and Pam had traveled. Evidently, Pam had walked right through their midst and they had not seen her—a huge drop of a miracle!

"He who dwells in the shelter of the Most High will rest in the shadow of the Almighty." (Ps. 91:1)

CHAPTER 31

Bib Overalls

When we pulled out of the driveway of Elaine's parents' home, some of the anxiety about the beginning of our venture back to Guatemala began to dissipate. We had said all our goodbyes, and after the first few miles we began to feel the reassurance of the Father's will in our lives.

The first leg of our journey would lead us through the so-called Skyline Drive through the Shenandoah Mountains of West Virginia, with the beautifully scenic views of the Shenandoah Valley. I really felt good about getting through Washington, DC and onto this first leg of the many miles we had to travel. Beautiful scenery and fresh mountain air almost made me forget the sweeping and sometimes tight mountainous curves and that I was pulling a trailer.

My world was about to be shaken.

Rounding one of the curves, I noticed a motor home that was coming toward us with some unusual appendages hanging out of the passenger-side door's window. I thought for a moment that the door might actually be open. There were a lot of body parts hanging out of that window. What I saw as we got closer was a cluster of arms and hands and a head. The arms and hands were frantically flapping and waving. As we passed each other, I distinctly heard the word *fire*. My first thought was that it couldn't be us and must be someone behind us. I glanced in the rearview mirror, and I actually saw smoke coming from *our* trailer!

Don't panic, Don, I thought. *Just get off the road as quick as you can.*

The next curve up ahead had a small rest-stop area, and I pulled off as close to the tree line as I could and jumped out. Sure enough, smoke was coming from the trailer. I quickly observed the situation and realized that the trailer tires were smoking. The trailer fenders were resting on top of the tires!

The school workshop had wanted to do a first-class job and put some fancy fenders on the trailer. They sure made it look like a class act. However, they did not take into consideration the way a missionary was going to pack. Missionaries' philosophy is, "There is always room for something else."

The workshop students had put some good leaf springs off the axle on the trailer, but what we really needed were extra heavy-duty, super hefty springs. When that last item was placed in the trailer, it tilted the capacity level over the top. The springs began to sag and let the fenders rest on top of the tires. I had not noticed this when we drove off from Elaine's parents' home. Thus, the constant friction of the tires rubbing on the fenders set the tires to smoking. They were not on fire, but you know the old saying: "Where there is smoke, there is fire." Believe me, we were close. They were smoldering, and I guess within a few more miles they would have been some balls of fire. Thankfully we were stopped in time!

With a little more investigating, I discovered that the fenders were an entity in themselves and were outside the framework of the trailer. That is to say, if I could get rid of the fenders, it would not affect the integrity of the support and function of the trailer and there would be no obstruction to the tires.

I had a dilemma. What did I have to help me get rid of those fenders? I remembered that I had picked up an old small hatchet and put it in the trailer. *Well,* I thought, *I could use that to hack through the sheet metal, but it would be quite a job.* My thoughts became vocal, and I said to my family, "Boy, if I had a crowbar, I could get rid of the fenders."

Just then we looked off to the edge of the woods. There, standing by the woods in bib overalls, was a West Virginia mountain man. And guess what he had in his hands—a crowbar! He approached me and said, "Son, if you won't hold me accountable for any overt damage, I can get rid of those fenders for you."

I said, "You've got all the disclaimers you need. Go ahead!"

And go ahead he did. *Bang, bang, slash, slash, rip, tear*—and the fenders were gone! There was just a pile of metal there at the rest stop. I gathered up the metal, and when I turned to thank him, he was gone. I will tell you what is not gone—it is the remembrance of that moment. It is burned in my memory! I call that a drop of a miracle!

CHAPTER 32

Stretch Out Your Hand

How can I pay tribute to all the medical personnel—all the surgeons, doctors, nurses, dentists, anesthetists, and support personnel—who so unselfishly came to Guatemala to serve and to give of their talent and time? Let me tell you one story.

Dr. Christian Helmus from Grand Rapids, Michigan, who was a specialist in head and neck surgery, came to Guatemala and performed many operations in the Chichicastenango Good Samaritan Hospital. He became concerned about the many young people in a few areas of the state of Quiche who had cases of cleft palate. This was one area he concentrated on, and he brought new life and a new level of self-image to many young people. Of course, he did many other operations, including tonsillectomies for our two boys, Don and Paul.

I tried on various occasions to get him to come to Nebaj. One day he finally consented, and I hurried back to our town to share the news. The message quickly spread throughout our area. When Dr. Chris arrived, the street in front of the clinic was lined with people.

A young Ixil boy by the name of Tomas was among the crowd. He was from a village that was about an eight-hour walk away. When it finally became Tomas's turn for a consultation, we got his story. His father and mother shared that Tomas would have seizures. One night during one of his seizures, he was thrown into the kitchen fire on the floor. Before they could rescue him, his left hand was severely burned. There was not much available in terms of a first response for treatment. We wondered how it had healed without infection. The healing resulted in a web-like structure stuck to all four fingers. It also went up the side of the thumb so that his hand looked like a duck's webbed foot. Tomas could only extend his hand about 10 percent, so he had no grip or use of his fingers. A year had gone by since the incident, and Tomas was now fourteen.

Dr. Chris took a look at Tomas's hand, and I could sense his brilliant mind began to form a plan. He called me to translate for the boy and his parents. Dr. Chris explained that he planned to cut the skin away from the fingers and thumb to set them free. Then he said that he would graft skin on to the newly formed hand. He then took a ballpoint pen and drew around all the areas that he planned on cutting and reforming. We prepared for the surgery. Dr. Chris's nurse was in attendance, as well as our Guatemalan nurse, dona Eloise. The painkillers were injected, and the surgery began.

It was an amazing procedure to watch. Dr. Chris's hands moved so perfectly, glided so calmly, and controlled without a hint of a twitch. Miraculous, blessed, and gifted hands gently coaxed a web less hand to appear. The fingers were free! Thin slices of skin were peeled from under Tomas's forearm and patched in place to make the grafts. Antibiotics, sutures, and bandages completed the task. Then the healing, therapy, and recuperation began.

Dr. Chris and his team stayed for one more day and then returned to the hospital in Chichicastenago. A few days later, they were on their way to the States.

Tomas was a good patient. He showed up every morning. Soon the stitches came out and the bandages came off. Several weeks of physical therapy followed, during which he squeezed a knitted ball (out of the missionary barrel), and then a few more weeks he worked with a more resistant ball. Then came the day when he could open and close his hand completely. He could grip things and throw a rock. And then he went home!

"Stretch forth your hand, Thomas!" Your God has done a great thing through His servants!

Bless them, our Father, those who bring healing and comfort to us in such an unselfish, committed, and servanthood way. Continue to gift them to bring glory to the kingdom of Jesus in this chaotic world. Amen and amen.

CHAPTER 33

Lest We Forget

We would like to pay tribute to all of those who stood with us. We know, beyond a shadow of a doubt, that we would not have had a ministry without the support of the Primitive Methodist Conference. That conference of local churches, pastors, and people made it possible.

The International Mission of the Primitive Methodist Church in the United States of America was the key to affirming our call. Perhaps when you think of it, maybe they took a chance. Possibly all the qualifications that they were looking for were not there. But there was no such thing as chance with this board. They were men and women filled with the Spirit! Before they made a decision, they bathed it and, yes, immersed it in prayer. They waited on His guidance and affirmation. They wanted God the Father's good, acceptable, and perfect will. Who would not want to be under a board like that? And decide they did—they appointed and commissioned us as missionaries under the Primitive Methodist Conference, and our field of ministry would be Guatemala, in Central America. Wonder of wonders, we were on our way!

Who could have orchestrated such events, blessings, and adventures? The conference stood with us with an array of support. At times we felt that we had our own private director, our own private treasurer, and our own private secretary, such was the personal touch. On top of all of that, each member of every church brought such a sense of unity behind us that we were awestruck.

We were humbled beyond belief. They were actually supporting us to do this! It was beyond our wildest dreams.

Sometimes they made us feel like some kind of a hero. But the reality is that they were the real heroes. Without fanfare they stood with us—in prayer, with financial support, with encouragement, and in a ton of other ways. They were a great influence on our lives, and their dedication challenged us. After visiting them we always returned to the mission field with new vigor and resolve. We were in it together. What a blessing! What a team! How could we possibility measure their worth to us? Their passion was contagious.

There were no mega-churches among them, but united they turned the world upside down. And they are still doing it!

Vive the Primitive Methodists!

Amen.

CHAPTER 34

A Lesson in Humility

Many issues and challenges came up in the new churches. Some of them were the church's complaints, accountability, and their relationship to the national conference and its authority and government. Some other concerns would also surface, such as outreach, discipleship programs, pastoral relations, disgruntled members, and other anxieties that would directly affect the local church. I think you can appreciate that there was as an array of challenges.

In order to address some of these issues, the national conference initiated a program called the overseeing pastor. They called the pastor or pastors in the program the Pastor Vigilante. It carried the feeling of watchful care. The vigilant pastor, or the overseeing pastor, would visit the churches in his area and, under the authority of the national conference, do his ministry, which consisted of a list of duties, such as mediating issues with the members of the congregation, settling issues with the pastors, affirming conference programs, encouraging the congregations, and advising on spiritual issues and doctrine. On occasion, when asked, the pastor would do some preaching. Obviously, there were other areas to be covered under this umbrella.

The program was designed to enhance the conference's

relationship to the churches and the churches' relationship to the conference, to encourage and affirm the churches, and to put out some fires before they got out of hand. The conference wanted to assure the churches of their autonomy and yet keep a sense of unity to the body of the conference. Needless to say, it was a challenging position.

I was appointed Pastor Vigilante for a few years in our area of Ixil country. I cannot recall how many churches were involved, but it was quite a few. I tried to be conscientious about the position and entered into it with somewhat of a fear and trembling.

I was a lot younger then, and I tried not to let the position put its charm on me. I did not want to come across as presenting that holier-than-thou attitude. I did not want there ever to be the feeling that I was looking down on anyone or carrying a proud arrogance. Perhaps I had drifted a little toward the privileged ego trip because I was beginning to feel a bit above some of the situations. I had begun to lose some of my sensitivity to some people and the issues. I was yanked back hard into the arena of the humbled.

One of the churches under my wing was in the coffee plantation called San Francisco. The church had gone through various pastors. The pastor who was there at the time I went actually lived and worked on the plantation. He and his wife also had a small store and small area where they served food (*comedor*).

We had visited the plantation on various occasions and had taken our mobile clinic there also, so I had contact with the church. I felt comfortable in being received there as the overseeing pastor.

Before this visit I am about to share, I had heard some rumors that some of the members of the church were a little dissatisfied with the leadership of the church, namely the pastor. I had known the pastor for a good while, had some good talks with him, and had eaten in his comedor on various occasions. I found it hard to believe that there could be any issues with him. Nevertheless, I decided to visit the church and smooth any ruffled feathers.

I arrived at the plantation and did a little visiting with some members to get a feel for any issues. Then it was time for the church service. The service ran its usual course, and then it was time for the message (sermon). Immediately, I knew what was wrong. The pastor spoke in such a low tone that his message was hardly audible. *My goodness,* I thought. *Speak up, my man! I think he is in dire need of some public speaking lessons. No wonder there is a problem here!*

I decided to stay overnight and discuss the church issues in the morning. I asked some of the elders and any members who could attend to meet early in the morning at the church. Bright and early the next morning, quite a group gathered to meet. I glanced across the group and surmised that they were pretty much the voice of the church. The pastor decided not to attend because he thought that the people might feel freer to share. After all, the vigilant pastor was present, and he could cure all ills.

I got right to the issue. I shared that I thought that they might need a new pastor. Maybe the present pastor could go on to be an elder and the conference could arrange to get a new man here. I could tell that my suggestion did not go over well. A lot of discussions went on among them. I spoke a little more about my feelings. Then, I realized there was a completely different atmosphere and attitude about our discussion.

One of the women rose to speak. She lived and worked on the plantation and had done her share of coffee-bean picking. She carried an aura of respect, and here is what she said: "You don't understand, pastor. You don't understand how much he loves us!"

At that moment, something triggered in me and I began to weep—end of the discussion, end of the issues, end of the meeting.

I got into the Land Rover and cried all the way home. That was a lot of crying. But it cleaned up my soul and got my sensitivity back. Thank you. Thank you, Spirit of the living God. Oh, what the drops of a miracle can do to you and for you.

CHAPTER 35

The Best Laid Plans of Mice and Men

The civil war in Guatemala began to take its toll. We experienced with our people the heartache and heartbreak of tragedy, terror, and death. The situation was beginning to deteriorate and become chaotic. We all began to become suspicious of one another. Security and stability became marginal. We were in hard times, and yet the churches were growing. We were experiencing a new depth of spiritual growth.

On various occasions during our local church services in Nebaj, the pastor would announce that don Donaldo (me) was taking a trip to visit some churches in the mountains. Then he would pray and ask who would like to accompany me. Various men would stand up. We knew they were literally sticking their necks out for us!

We began to survey the reality and felt that we were becoming a liability to our people. We decided that we should put a game plan together. We made a decision that when the time came that we were jeopardizing the safety of our Ixil people, we would leave our beloved Ixil country.

The EGP made the decision for us.

We got a letter in the mail one day with the return address of a church in Guatemala that I did not recognize. I opened the envelope and found a letter from the EGP. It had the logo of Che Guevara on the letterhead. In essence, it read, "Senor Donald Lawrence, you have been tried and found guilty of collaborating with the Guatemalan government under the disguise of a CIA spy. You cannot fool the people with your good works. Señor Lawrence, the EGP informs you that you will be executed. We give you 24 hours for you and your family to leave Nebaj, after receiving this message, and 48 hours to go from Guatemala. If you do not do this the ARMY will fulfill its orders."

The next twenty-four hours were a blur. It is amazing how much you can get done! We packed some barrels, said teary goodbyes, had a preaching service in the middle of the street with one of the barrels as a pulpit, and left everything involving the churches and congregations in the hands of the Holy Spirit. Our great friend and colleague Gale Morris arrived to help us pack and transport some stuff. Two ambulances with some of the volunteers showed up. They escorted us out of town with one ambulance in the front and one in the rear of our mini convoy. They escorted us all the way to Chichicastenango. The next day Bill Vasey, who was the field director, took over in the capital and made all the arrangements to fly us out of Guatemala.

Guess who was there to meet us when we got off the plane at 3:30 a.m. in Maryland—Joe and Pat Morrone! They took us in again, and we were to begin a new journey with Jesus.

Early Days in Ixil Country

Forging the rivers to spread the "Good News"

Some Members of the congregation in Ilom

No street named after me, but I did get a bumper

Returning from a visit to some congregations in Ixil Country

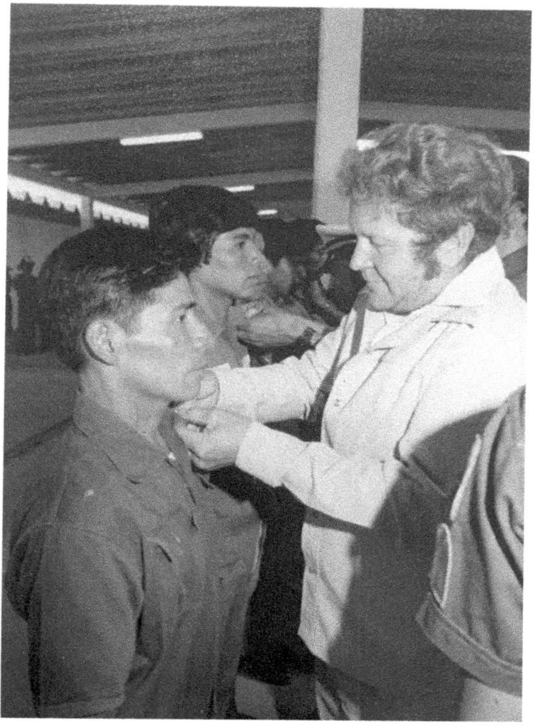

Ixil evangelist Luis receiving his pin for graduating from the firefighter course

Baptisms

Nan Cat with daughter and son

Baptisms

Another ambulance – this time for Chajul

ABOUT THE AUTHOR

Blinding lights still occur.

Suddenly, there was a blinding, brilliant light that flashed from the sky, a voice rolled from heaven, and then a man fell to the ground. That short phrase described some of the visible aspects of the rather sudden and dramatic moments when the apostle Paul had his encounter with the Lord Jesus Christ. Paul's encounter with Christ Jesus, of course, happened over two thousand years ago, and I guess the question that haunts us today is, are the blinding lights and the voice from heaven and the dramatic conversions and the encounters with Christ Jesus still happening today? I write today to contend to and to attest to the fact that Almighty God our Father is still at work in the world today!

I was raised in what might be considered a nominally Christian home. I was exposed to the Gospel and the light of Jesus. However, it never developed. It was as if I loved darkness. It was as the saying goes: I had eyes to see but I could not see, had ears to hear but could not hear. I was blind, deaf, and dead spiritually. I was locked in the prison of me, myself, and I. It was going to take a supernatural touch to unlock and release the divine splendor. It took a chain of events to make that happen.

When I returned from Korea, I was assigned to a base on Cape Cod, Massachusetts. My wife and I moved to the area, and this assignment was to become a turning point in my life. Three families began to play a significant role in my life: my landlord and his wife; a

New Bedford, Massachusetts, police detective and his wife; and the Primitive Methodist pastor and his wife. These people demonstrated dynamic Christianity in action. Of course, there were other aspects that pulled and pointed me toward Christ Jesus. The church people were praying for me, and I had begun to read the Bible. Slowly, I was coming under the conviction of the Holy Spirit, and to be quite frank I was becoming disturbed and uncomfortable.

My wife began to press me in her own way. One day in my frustration, I said to her, “Okay, give me just two weeks and I will find out something wrong in the lives of these ‘fanatics.’” Two weeks passed, and I was unable to come up with anything. Their close walk with the Lord showed through even under scrutiny. Then I knew that I must make a decision. Either I must start back or say no!

So, one day I started back. I returned from the base early one morning and said to my wife, “I have a strange feeling that something is going to happen. Take off from work, and let’s go for a ride.” We rode to a beach on the Massachusetts coast. It was a beautiful late October day, and the beach was deserted. We began to walk among the sand dunes and onto the beach, and then, suddenly, it happened. There was a blinding light from above that outshined the sun, and I fell to my knees. I seemed to be surrounded by and immersed in this aura of indescribable love, and I wept as I had never wept before in my life. I did not fully realize what was happing to me at that moment, but I did know that I was experiencing an unbelievable feeling of forgiveness of sin and reassurance. A few hours later, when we returned to New Bedford, I sought out my pastor. When I shared with him my experience, he said, “Don, what you experienced was what Jesus calls the new birth, or as we say, you were born again!”

Now, I do not know why I had to experience such a dazzling encounter with the Father. Maybe it is because those who are the farthest away need the most dramatic way to be brought back. I do know that the parable of the prodigal son has special meaning to me (Luke 15:11–31). I started back and my Father ran to meet me. I also know this: God meets each one of us as we are. We are all different. We are made up of different personalities, characters, and backgrounds, and God knows this and loves each one of us in such a special way! God knew and knows how I am made up, and I accept the fact that He knew just the kind of encounter I needed that day.

Since then, I have come to realize that the important thing is not the manner of the encounter—whether it is intense, or dazzling, or the still small voice—but that there *is* an encounter. And not an encounter only, but that we experience the forgiveness of sins, that we are ushered into a personal relationship with Jesus, and that we go on to live with Him and for Him filled with the Holy Spirit.

That day on the beach, I had a new perspective on life when I got up from my knees. Not only were the blues bluer and the greens greener, but a mission and a challenge were embodied in the experience. I do not consider myself in the same class with the apostle Paul, and I stand in awe that God can use me. I have had to grow each day in my Christian walk and still have a long way to go, and as Paul did, I press on.

The story goes on. I went off to Nyack Missionary College, on to Guatemala into Ixil country as a missionary of the Good News under the International Mission Board of the Primitive Methodist Church; worked in the Chester County Migrant Ministry (Outreach Coordinator); served as pastor of Lionville Community Methodist Church in Lionville, Pennsylvania, under the Primitive Methodist Conference; and also became a worker at H-E-B Grocery in Texas. Each of those has a story that maybe I shall write about someday.

Yes, Almighty God our Father is still at work in the world today dropping those "drops of a miracle". Praise His Holy Name!

Lightning Source UK Ltd.
Milton Keynes UK
UKHW012209161020
371737UK00007B/321/J

9 781664 202719